OLIVER CROMWELL

AND HIS WARTS

by Alan MacDonald

Illustrated by Philip Reeve

Scholastic Children's Books,
Euston House, 24 Eversholt Street,
London NW1 1DB, UK

A division of Scholastic Ltd
London ~ New York ~ Toronto ~ Sydney ~ Auckland
Mexico City ~ New Delhi ~ Hong Kong

Published in the UK by Scholastic Ltd, 2000

10 digit ISBN 0 439 99610 4
13 digit ISBN 978 0439 99610 5

Typeset by M Rules
Printed in the UK by CPI Bookmarque, Croydon, CR0 4TD

19 20 18

Contents

INTRODUCTION

Which dead famous person gets their big head in a million photos every year?

QUEEN VICTORIA

DARREN SQUIGLEY OF CLASS 3B, SPUD ROAD MIDDLE SCHOOL, PONGCHESTER

CLUE: IT'S THIS ONE

OLIVER CROMWELL

The answer's dead obvious really, since this is a book about Oliver Cromwell. Oliver gets his picture taken so often because his statue stands right outside the Houses of Parliament in London. (It's often used by the pigeons for target practice.)

You'd think that having your statue outside Westminster would mean that you're pretty popular. But the fact is that many people still can't stand Ollie – even though he's been dead for over 300 years! When the Westminster statue was first unveiled it was done early in the morning for fear of creating a stink. The stink followed anyway. In 1953 someone poured five gallons of smelly creosote over the statue.

So why is Oliver so unpopular? For a start he's known as the father of British Parliament. (So he's got a lot to answer for.) But he probably didn't win too many friends by chopping off a king's head. The British tend to be fond of their royals but not of their revolutionaries.

You won't find Oliver in any list of kings and queens, yet for five years he ran the country. Some people claim he was a big-headed tyrant, others that he was a great man. This book won't settle all the arguments, but it will tell you some of the fascinating facts that history books leave out. Such as why you might find Oliver at a football match, how he caused a big stink at a party, and why his head kept popping up long after he was buried.

As you sneak a look at Oliver's undiscovered diaries and learn the truth about prim Puritans and dashing Cavaliers you'll find out how Oliver became a Roundhead revolutionary. Read on for a gripping tale full of battles, beheadings and unbelievably big noses, and meet the real Oliver Cromwell – warts and all!

TIMELINE:
OLIVER THE OBSCURE

1599: OLIVER CROMWELL BORN IN HUNTINGDON, CAMBRIDGESHIRE.

1600: CHARLES I BORN IN SCOTLAND.

1603: GOOD QUEEN BESS (LIZ I) KICKS THE BUCKET. JAMES VI OF SCOTLAND ADDS ENGLAND TO HIS CROWN COLLECTION.

1616-17: OLIVER GOES TO CAMBRIDGE – AND SPENDS MOST OF HIS TIME PLAYING FOOTBALL.

1620: OLIVER AND GIRLFRIEND ELIZABETH MARRY – AND START RAISING A BIG FAMILY.

1625: JAMES I PEGS OUT. CHARLES I BECOMES KING OF ENGLAND.

1628: OLIVER ELECTED AS MP FOR HUNTINGDON.

1629: CHARLES GIVES PARLIAMENT THE BOOT AND DOES WITHOUT ONE FOR 11 YEARS.

M.P.s? WHO NEEDS THEM?

1631: BAD NEWS – OLLIE FALLS ON HARD TIMES.

BANK STATEMENT You're skint.

1636: GOOD NEWS! RICH UNCLE DIES AND OLIVER COMES INTO PROPERTY.

R.I.P. RICH UNCLE

1640: OLLIE M.P SITS IN THE LONG PARLIAMENT.

HOW LONG DOES THIS GO ON FOR?

ZzzZZz

1642: THE GRAND REMONSTRANCE — PARLIAMENT'S BIG WHINGE. CHARLES BOTCHES ARREST OF FIVE REBEL M.P.s

YOU'RE NICKED! HANG ON – WHERE'D THEY ALL GO?

22 AUGUST 1642: CIVIL WAR IS DECLARED! CAPTAIN CROMWELL JOINS ROUNDHEADS.

I DECLARE THIS CIVIL WAR OPEN!

SNIP!

KID CROMWELL - A COUNTRY LIFE

Oliver Cromwell may have ended up a king-crunching revolutionary, a military genius and the only dictator in English history, but he started off as a farmer. No one had even heard of Cromwell before he was 40 years old.

(Most 40-year-olds in seventeenth century England were thinking about their funeral arrangements. Not Oliver, he was just getting started.)

Oliver Cromwell was born on 25 April 1599. His mum and dad named him Oliver after his rich and famous Uncle Ollie. (More of him later.)

Only a year and a half after our Oliver, another baby was born. His name was Charles and he was the son of the next king of England – James I. Little Charlie would grow up to be Oliver's greatest enemy.

There is a story that young Ollie and Charles once met as kids and got into a fight. It's one of many tales about young Oliver's childhood. If we believe them all the kid Cromwell must have led a pretty hair-raising early life.

10

Most of these stories are probably mad myths that were invented about Oliver once he was dead famous. Only one story was told by Cromwell himself. In his childhood Oliver claimed a giantess once appeared to him in a vision and predicted he would do great things. Unfortunately when he told the story to his father, he got a great hiding for being such an almighty big-head. Young Oliver was right of course but that didn't save him.

The Cromwell clan

While Charles I was born into a royally famous family, no one would have guessed that young Oliver was going to make his mark in history. His dad, Robert Cromwell, had a farm in Huntingdon, a small town in Cambridgeshire. It was a middling kind of town and Robert was a middling, sensible kind of chap, neither rich nor poor. Robert was said to be 'a man of good sense'. As the second son, though, he missed out on his father's wealth which always went to the oldest brother. Robert Cromwell was active in local life as a judge, MP, and the 'Commissioner of Sewers'. Not so much a big noise as a big stink.

However Oliver's family did contain its share of interesting people, as a quick glance at his family album will prove.

11

Oliver's family album

Tough Thomas Cromwell (great-great-uncle)

The first famous Cromwell was Thomas, King Henry VIII's head hit-man. In 1535 Henry had a small cash flow problem (he'd spent all his money on gambling and going to war). He set Thomas Cromwell the job of reforming the monasteries. When Henry said 'reforming' what he actually meant was … well … robbing them. Henry's excuse was that they were all corrupt (unlike him, of course). Tough-nut Thomas was an ex-soldier and just the man for the job. He flattened hundreds of monasteries, booted out the monks and stole all their gold for the greedy king. This made Henry much richer and Thomas a big favourite. That is, until Tom made the mistake of suggesting the king take Anne of Cleves for his fourth wife. Henry thought Anne was as ugly as a horse and chopped off Thomas's tough nut in revenge.

Diamond Dick Cromwell (great-grandfather)

During the looting of the monasteries, Tom's nephew, Richard Cromwell, helped himself to their lands. But his big break came in 1540 when he took part in a royal joust in front of Henry VIII and stole the show. Clad in shining armour and mounted on a horse draped in white velvet, dashing Dick beat all comers. The king instantly declared himself a big fan and dropped a diamond ring off his finger with the words: 'Formerly thou wast my Dick, but hereafter you shalt be my diamond.' Luckily for Dick he was nimble enough to catch the king's diamond (otherwise he might have been known hereafter as butterfingers). From that day the king's diamond was added to the Cromwell family crest. He bagged a knighthood and founded the wealth of the Cromwell family.

Sheriff Sir Henry Cromwell (grandfather)

Not be outdone by his glittering father, 'Diamond Dick', Henry was known as 'the golden knight'. He married the daughter of a lord mayor of London and had Queen Elizabeth to dinner at his house. As the county sheriff he fought in the showdown

13

against the Spanish Armada – though it's unlikely he wore a silver star and a ten gallon hat.

Sir Oliver Cromwell (uncle)

Uncle Oliver was Henry's eldest son, so he got all Dad's goodies – like the big abbey, the estate, the family jewels, etc. When King James stayed at his house the Scottish monarch declared: 'Marry, mon, thou hast treated me better than any one syn I left Edinboro!' – which for non-Scots means, 'Great party, Ollie!' It's hardly surprising the new king enjoyed his stay. Oliver showered his visitor with gifts including: 'goodly horses, deep-mouthed hounds, hawks of excellent wing' and a cup of pure gold. No wonder James came back to visit again – and again and again.

That was the family Oliver was born into. Some of them were knights but, apart from Thomas Cromwell, none of them were exactly famous. No one expected much of Oliver when he was born either. He was the fifth child and the second boy in the family. His elder brother Henry died when Oliver was a teenager, so Oliver only had his sisters – all six of them! You can probably imagine what this must have been like. Maybe it's the reason Oliver was so bossy in later life.

Hairy schooldays

Little is known about young Ollie's childhood. Since he didn't do anything remarkable in his first 40 years no one took much notice of him. What we do know can only be pieced together from stories and guesswork.

If the tales are true he was a bit of a tearaway. He rode horses, skipped off school, broke down hedges and stole doves from his dad's farm. At school he certainly wasn't teacher's pet. More than once he got a sound whipping from his teacher (especially when he boasted he was destined for greatness). Schooldays in the seventeenth century could be cruel. For instance here are the punishments a teacher could hand out at one school:

The school drew the line at clouting pupils on the head, presumably in case it knocked out any brains they had!

If you think you have it hard at school, listen to what young Oliver had to put up with. At around seven years old he started attending the local grammar school in Huntingdon. It had only one tiny classroom and just one teacher, called Dr Beard.

Oliver went to Dr Beard for lessons beginning at six in the morning and ending *twelve* long hours later. On Sundays, as a special treat, young Ollie got the day off to go to church and listen to the minister's sermon. Who was the minister? None other than his dear old teacher, Dr Beard again.

Oliver's teacher was a devout Puritan. We'll meet the Prim Puritans later. For now let's just say Dr Beard was famous for writing a book called: *The Theatre of God's Judgments, translated from the French and augmented with over 300 examples*. We can safely say there weren't many jokes in it!

At school the main subject wasn't maths or English, it was RE (religious education). Oliver would have been expected to learn large chunks of the Bible off by heart. Next on the timetable came the Classics – Latin, Greek and Hebrew – which he was taught to read, write and speak. Logic (the art of clear thinking and argument) and Rhetoric (the art of speaking in public) were also essential for a rounded education. One little boy in Oliver's time could 'perfectly read any of the English, Latin, French or Gothic letters, pronouncing the first three languages exactly'. Not bad, especially as he was only two and a half!

It's a lock-out

It all sounds pretty dull, but once a year there was a chance for schoolkids to get their own back on their teachers. This wonderful custom was called 'barring out' and you might want to try a historical re-enactment:

1. SHUT THE DOOR OF THE CLASSROOM AND LOCK IT.
SLAM! click!

2. WHEN YOUR TEACHER BANGS ON THE DOOR TELL HER... YOU'RE BARRED!
KNOCK! KNOCK!

3. PRESENT HER WITH A LIST OF YOUR DEMANDS.
3B
1 FREE CHOCOLATE
2 7-DAY WEEKENDS
3 NO SKOOL DINNER

4. WHEN SHE GIVES IN—AND ONLY THEN— OPEN THE DOOR.

Of course 'barring out' could get out of hand. At King Edward School in Birmingham in 1667, for instance, the 'barring out' turned into an all-out riot. Stones were thrown, windows were smashed and the school wall was reduced to rubble. The schoolkids were having such a riot that local hooligans came from the town to join in. From then on the school governors put a ban on 'barring out'.

It's a pity we don't know whether Oliver Cromwell's school in Huntingdon allowed the custom. It's difficult to imagine anyone locking the door on strict Dr Beard with his birch in his hand.

Unruly students

Oliver himself didn't show any sign of being a genius, but when he was 17 he did go on to Cambridge University. As a student, it's said, he was more interested in mucking around with his mates than studying his books. There is a story that he once jumped from the window of his first floor college room on to a horse standing outside. Oliver thought it was a great joke, but we don't know what the horse thought.

Students in Oliver's day weren't treated any better than schoolboys. The President of Trinity College, Oxford – the daftly named Dr Kettle – used to peep through keyholes to check if his students were working. Another of his odd habits was carrying a pair of scissors with him at all times. Dr Kettle got very steamed up about long hair and if he saw a hairy student, he gave them a quick trim as he went past. Once, when he didn't have his scissors with him, he even used a bread knife!

Whippings were just as common. One student called John Milton had to change his tutor at Cambridge because the whippings became a sore point. (Funnily enough Milton would grow up to be a famous poet and a great favourite of Oliver's.)

Oliver himself probably took his fair share of punishments. At Cambridge he had a reputation for being 'one of the chief match makers and players of football'. In those days football was rather different from the game we know today. One Puritan compared it to 'a friendlie kind of fight' – and that was putting it mildly! Sides could number as many as a hundred and there were no rules except trying to get the ball from one end of 'the pitch' to the other. You could kick, grab or punch the ball – or your opponent if they got in your way. It wasn't unusual for windows to get broken, not to mention legs, arms and noses.

Cromwell's passion for football wouldn't raise an eyebrow today, but his tutors probably didn't approve. You can imagine what his end of term report might have looked like:

UNIVERSITY TERM REPORT

SUBJECT: Oliver Cromwell
COLLEGE: Sidney Sussex, Cambridge
TUTOR: Dr Birchem.

RELIGION	Lord help us!
LATIN	Patheticus, Patheticum.
GREEK	No hero.
HEBREW	Slapdash.
SCIENCE	Woeful.
MATHEMATICS	If Oliver breaks five windows at a cost of one shilling each, how much does he owe the College!
LANGUAGE	Shocking, especially on the football field.
FOOTBALL	Outstanding. Sidney Sussex 1st XXI Captain. Strike rate: 2 black eyes, 3 nosebleeds, one dislocated shoulder.
WRESTLING	See football.

TUTOR'S COMMENTS: Oliver has a rough and blustering nature. He has as much chance of making his mark on history as football has of becoming a sport watched by millions. T. Birchem.

The college that Oliver attended was known as 'a hot-bed of Puritanism'. Religion was a battlefield in the seventeenth century. In fact it was religion that helped to start the Civil War. Anglicans disliked Roman Catholics, who were hated by Puritans, who in turn were sneered at by Anglicans. It could all get a bit confusing. To help you sort it all out here's a quick guide to the main armies … er … religious parties.

WARTS AND ALL - WARRING RELIGIONS

NAME	TOP BANANA	KEY BELIEFS
ANGLICANS	THE KING	NATIONAL CHURCH HEADED BY BISHOPS UNDER THE KING'S THUMB.
ROMAN CATHOLICS	THE POPE	LOYAL TO CHURCH AND POPE IN ROME.
PURITANS	NO ONE	WANTED SIMPLE SERVICES WITHOUT 'POPISH' PRACTICES, AND NO NATIONAL CHURCH.
PRESBYTERIANS	CHURCH ASSEMBLY	WANTED A NATIONAL CHURCH BUT NO INTERFERING KING OR BISHOPS THANK YOU.

Prim Puritans

The Puritans were a major influence on their age and also on young Cromwell. When someone's called a 'Puritan' today it usually means they're prim or po-faced. This has its roots in the gloomy attitude of many Puritans in Oliver's time.

The name 'Puritan' actually started out as an insult. In Elizabethan times one Puritan complained...

It was little better than being called a bloodsucker.

The name actually came from the Puritan desire to 'purify' the Church of England of all traces of Catholicism. By the reign of Charles I Puritans were an influential group who included many of the leading figures in Parliament (like John Hampden, the leader of the Commons).

Puritans believed that worship in church should be simple, solemn and without fuss and ceremony. There were lots of things they didn't approve of. For example:

THE POPE

BISHOPS

THE SIGN OF THE CROSS USED IN BAPTISMS

GIVING A RING IN MARRIAGE

PRIESTS DRESSING UP IN NICE COLOURFUL ROBES

CHRISTMAS

Later, when Oliver ruled the country, Puritans got their chance to make England a more gloomy place. But during the reign of Charles I many Puritans despaired of England altogether and set sail for new lands where they could follow their beliefs in peace. In 1620 the Pilgrim Fathers boarded the Mayflower and sailed to New England in America. Other families later joined them and created a whole fun-loving new way of life.

The story goes that Cromwell himself considered hopping on a boat to America but the Civil War came along and changed his mind.

Man about the house

When Oliver had only been at Cambridge for a year something happened which changed his life. His father, Robert Cromwell, died. This meant the end of Oliver's idle life as a student. No more kicking his friends on the football field for him. It was back to Huntingdon to become head of the Cromwell household.

In those days the head of the house was always a man. It didn't matter that Ollie was only 18 and three of his sisters were older. Since his brother Henry had died, he was the only man of the house. Oliver was now responsible for running the farm and keeping his mum and sisters. It was a lot to ask of a wild teenager whose main achievement up to now was organizing college footie matches.

Young Ollie wasn't up to the job and quickly went to the dogs. Stories say he spent most of the time with his pals gambling, running up bills, ordering drinks and forgetting to pay for them. If the tales are to be believed he also loved practical jokes. Here's one stinky tale he'd have recorded in his diary if he'd ever kept one.

Oliver's Secret Diary

20th December 1618

Party at Uncle Oliver's up at Hinchinbrooke House. Mother said I must go even though they're so dull I could fall asleep standing up. Decided to dream up some mischief to amuse myself and my pals. Told my mother and sisters to go on ahead without me, while I put stage one of my plan into operation. Wearing my best doublet and jacket I went to the cow field and covered my clothes in foul smelling poo. I stank to high heaven, but that was all part of my hilarious joke.

Soon after, I presented myself at Uncle's house. The music and dancing were already under way. After a few mugs of ale I desired my Lady Westwood to dance with me. It wasn't long before she realized where the foul stink was coming from — ME! She tried to escape but I held her so tight that,

> I confess, much of the dung rubbed off on her! I danced with several other women and (how I laughed!) succeeded in fouling their clothes too. Soon the stink was exceeding great throughout the room and my uncle was called. Can you believe he had me chucked in the duck-pond to clean me off? What's the matter with the old goat? Can't he take a joke?

The tale of young Oliver daubing himself with poo for a party seems hard to believe. Is this the man who would later rule all England, Scotland and Ireland? The story could be made up but it does fit with later stories about Oliver's character. All his life he had a love of rude practical jokes. Pillow fights, flicking ink, stealing wigs – Oliver loved any kind of horse-play. History has often painted him as a prim Puritan, but in some ways Oliver was the Dennis the Menace of his day.

For now, Cromwell was young and hardly dreamed of becoming dead famous. Yet important events were soon to call him away from Huntingdon and into Parliament. The rough-mannered farmer with his rude jokes would soon start to attract attention in higher circles.

ANGRY OLIVER AND THE REBEL PARLIAMENT

At the age of 21, Oliver put his wild days behind him and got married in 1620. His bride was Elizabeth Bouchier, the daughter of a rich London fur trader. Elizabeth was the oldest of six children and was two years older than Oliver. She was a gentle, homely kind of girl. She may not have been a great beauty but then, let's face it, nor was our Oliver.

Oliver and Elizabeth settled down to a quiet life in Huntingdon looking after their land and starting a family. They had more luck with the family than the land. Their family album needed extra wide pages.

Mrs Cromwell

It's no wonder Elizabeth Cromwell was known as quiet and modest. She had eight children and on average she got pregnant every other year. She can't have had much energy left for living it up!

In Puritan times a wife was meant to obey her husband as her master, bring up her children and manage her house. Housework meant more than the odd bit of

27

dusting. According to a book called *The English Housewife* a Puritan wife's talents were supposed to include:

> *Skill in Physick* [medicine], *surgery, cookery, extraction of oils, banqueting stuff, ordering of great feasts, preserving of all sorts of wines ... distillations of perfumes, ordering of wool, hemp or flax, making cloth and dyeing, knowledge of dairies, the office of malting of oats, their excellent uses in family brewing, baking and all things belonging to a household.*

If Mrs Cromwell managed that lot on top of eight children she must have been some woman. Whatever her talents, she and Oliver were a happy pair. Later when Oliver was an important general he always found time to write home.

Unfortunately as Oliver's family got bigger his family fortune got smaller. When his father died Cromwell could count himself a country gentleman. But by 1631 when Oliver sold the farm in Huntingdon and moved to St Ives he was no more than a mere yeoman. But what is a yeoman?

WARTS AND ALL – LORDS AND COMMONERS

Society in the seventeenth century was shaped like a pyramid. The king sat on top with the stinking poor at the bottom. In between came aristocrats, gentlemen, merchants and yeomen.

These different groups could be quickly told apart by their clothes and their houses. A yeoman might have a ten room house, glass in his windows and furniture in his rooms. By comparison a poor country labourer might own a smoky two-roomed hut made out of sticks, mud and cow-dung… and they were the lucky ones! Anyone out of work had to beg or starve. Here's a woeful rhyme describing their plight:

> No meat, no drink, no lodging but the floor
> No stool to sit, no lock upon the door,
> No straw to make a litter* at night,
> Nor any candlestick to hold the light.

Young Cromwell must have been horrified when he heard that even the aristocratic branch of his family had fallen on hard times. His uncle Oliver was so skint that he was having to sell his mansion house at Hinchbrooke. Sir Oliver must have regretted the night he feasted King James royally. The sponging king had come back so many times that his host was now practically broke. Times were hard too for young Oliver and his family – and the new king on the throne wasn't making life any easier.

* A litter was a bed.

Charles Almighty

James I died in 1625. People said the king had been 'the wisest fool in Christendom'. In other words James was clever but he didn't have an ounce of common sense. One of James's not so wise ideas was something called 'the divine right of kings'. James told his parliament:

> *Kings are God's lieutenants upon earth and sit upon God's throne.*

In practice this meant James believed he could do whatever he liked. After all, he was God's number one favourite! Some people felt 'the divine right of kings' was dreamed up by royalty to suit themselves.

WHAT ABOUT THE DIVINE RIGHT OF FARMERS?

BAAAA! HUMBUG!

When James died and Charles came to the throne, many people hoped that he would be different from his dopey dad. But Charles was a chip off the old block. His dad had taught him all about the divine right of kings and if anything Charles was even more big-headed. What he failed to recognize was that times had changed. In Tudor times Henry VIII could chop off the head of anyone who disagreed with him. In the Stuart age Parliament was no longer content to be the king's pet poodle. It was the struggle for power between king and Parliament that would lead to Civil War and the rise of Oliver Cromwell.

31

Charles would later become Ollie's greatest enemy, so now's a good time to take a closer look at both of them.

CHARLES 'ALMIGHTY' I

WANDERING EYES –TOO SHY TO LOOK YOU IN THE EYE

REGAL NOSE

DASHING MOUSTACHE AND PRINCELY POINTY BEARD

LONG, FLOWING LOCKS

KINGLY CLOTHES –SILKS AND LACE

SENSITIVE HANDS –MADE FOR MUSIC, ART AND POETRY (NOT FIGHTING WARS)

SMALL AND THIN

OLIVER CROMWELL

BLAZING EYES (WARNING: EASILY OFFENDED)

BIG NOSE

RUDDY COMPLEXION

NASTY WARTS

SHOULDER LENGTH HAIR

DETERMINED MOUTH

POWERFULLY BUILT

COUNTRY COUSIN CLOTHES

TALL FOR THE AGE – 1.75m (5ft 9)

32

Charles was, in many ways, Oliver's total opposite. Cromwell was rough, rude and – let's be honest – pretty ugly. Charles in contrast was rich, pampered, kingly and handsome. He'd also married a Catholic – Henrietta Maria – which had lots of his Protestant subjects worried. During his childhood Charles had to wear extra-strong boots to support his weak legs. As a grown-up he was a shy man with a high-pitched voice and a bit of a stammer. He tried to hide his shyness by acting tough but it probably didn't fool anyone. It's hard to sound tough when you've got a voice like Mickey Mouse.

The House of Cousins

In 1628 Cromwell was elected as one of the two MPs for Huntingdon. It was a logical step in his career. He already had nine cousins sitting in Parliament so it was a bit like being invited to a big family occasion (lots of speeches and very little fun).

Charles I had only been king for three years but he was already losing patience with Parliament. What Charles wanted was money. He'd stupidly got himself into a war with France and Spain. To be fighting two powerful countries was bad enough, but to make matters worse Charles entrusted his army to a walking disaster called the Duke of Buckingham. Buckingham's one talent was for losing his army as well as the battle. In an attack on the French port of La Rochelle his bungling led to the slaughter of over 4,000 Englishmen.

Yet Charles opened his next parliament (the one Cromwell attended) by demanding money for another attack on the French. Who would lead it? Bungling

Buckingham naturally. How do you think Parliament answered? 'Not on your nelly,' of course!

Charles was so mad at not getting the money he wanted that he gave Parliament the boot. (This would become a bad habit over the years.) Charles thought he could do without Parliament. He ruled by himself for the next 11 years. It's known in history books as the Eleven Years Tyranny.

Mad money making schemes

If Parliament wouldn't vote him taxes Charles would find other ways of raising cash. He set his advisers to work to think up crackpot laws which he could use to fill his piggy bank. Some of his schemes were unusual, others were plain bonkers.

Fine a knight

In medieval times any gentleman worth over £40 a year had to serve the king as a knight. Charles dug up this ancient law and decided to fine his subjects for 'failing to accept knighthoods'. This was every bit as batty as it sounds. Imagine our queen today saying to her subjects:

This is exactly what Charles did. Cromwell was one of those who had to pay up for not receiving an honour he didn't ask for in the first place. Batty! Of course, if anyone did accept a knighthood it came at a price, so the cunning king won both ways.

Play monopoly
Another trick the king used was the game of monopoly. In Charles's case this didn't involve buying Mayfair and building hotels (that Monopoly hadn't been invented). The monopolies Charles sold gave you the sole right to make or sell something. No one could set up in competition so you could name any price you liked. One of the most hated monopolies involved soap. It was hated because...

Predictably Charles ignored the protests and went on selling monopolies to his favourites.

Trespassers will be robbed
Another ancient law that Charles dusted down allowed him to fine anyone who trespassed on royal forest land. Sounds fair enough, but as usual there was a catch. In ancient times any open land where the king went hunting was 'royal' land. Charles ordered his advisors to search back 300 years in the record books to rediscover the ancient boundaries of his land. Amazingly he found

he owned a lot more land than he thought! He could then accuse lots of people of 'stealing' his land and charge them whacking great fines.

Shocking ship money

The most unpopular of Charles's batty taxes was ship money. In war-time the king had sometimes demanded 'ship money' from ports and coastal towns to help protect them with a strong navy. All well and good, but Charles extended the law so that the whole country had to pay ship money whether they lived in Bristol or Birmingham. People protested that England wasn't at war and there wasn't even a threat of war (not to mention the fact that Birmingham was miles from the sea). But Charles had an answer to that one – he declared a state of emergency because pirates had been sighted in the English Channel!

Cromwell himself was said to be 'a great stickler' against the mad tax.

In the end, all Charles's mad money-making schemes were doomed to failure. As the 11 years wore on, more and more people began to refuse to pay the king's batty taxes. Meanwhile Charles was borrowing wads of cash to pay for his expensive court and palaces. Eventually, in 1640, the king's empty piggy bank forced him to call Parliament again. Oliver Cromwell was among the MPs who returned to Westminster. Like the rest, he was in no mood to be helpful.

Puritan Oliver

What had Oliver been doing with himself during the 11 years Charles ruled without Parliament? Firstly he'd been struggling to support his rapidly growing family. Sadly his mother's brother had passed away in 1636.

WHAT SAD NEWS...

But in his will the uncle had left Oliver his house and estate in Ely, Cambridgeshire.

STILL, LIFE GOES ON, EH?

Oliver rose again to the status of gentleman and stopped having to count the pennies. He'd changed in other ways too. Somewhere in the early 1630s something happened to Oliver which changed his life. He had a religious conversion. For a long time Oliver made himself ill worrying that God wouldn't accept someone as rotten as him.

Oliver's secret diary.

__19th April 1629__

In great misery. Face covered in pimples. Skin dry and flaky. Rotten stomach-aches. Horrible headaches. I am the chief of sinners.

__1st May 1629__

Think I am dying. Can't rise from my bed. Can't sleep at night. Truly it would be a mercy if God put an end to my miserable existence. Oh, wretch that I am!

__17th July 1629__

WOE! MISERY! Etc. Etc. Etc.

Then, somewhere in his thirties, it all changed. Oliver became convinced he was one of God's 'elect' – which meant his place was booked in heaven. As you can imagine, that cheered him up. For the rest of his life, Oliver's Puritan beliefs would govern his every decision. He believed his rise to fame was all part of a great heavenly plan. Of course, this made him pretty difficult to argue with.

38

Odd isn't it? Both Oliver and Charles I believed that they were carrying out God's plan, yet they disagreed on almost everything.

Oliver was soon to meet other Puritans who felt that the country was going to the dogs. Parliament was swarming with them.

Revolting Parliament

When Charles I recalled Parliament in 1640, Puritans were among his strongest critics. The first parliament in England for ten years was called the Short Parliament. Why? Because it lasted precisely three weeks – that's how long it took for Charles to fall out with his MPs. The argument went like this.

The Short Parliament was followed later that year by the Long Parliament. This one got its name by lasting for a record-breaking 13 years, even through the Civil War. Oliver Cromwell was there at the start as an MP for Cambridge. He wasn't famous yet but it's clear he made an early impression.

Sir Philip Warwick, a royalist, witnessed Oliver's first big speech in Parliament. He wasn't impressed with the scruffy, hot-headed newcomer. Sir Philip was dapperly dressed, but he said Cromwell's plain cloth suit looked like it had been made by 'a bad country tailor'. His shirt was dirty and he even had a speck of blood at the collar. As for Oliver's hat, it didn't even have a hat-band! Warwick said Cromwell's face was 'swollen and reddish, his voice sharp and untunable'.

All in all Cromwell was a dog's breakfast, but it was his passion that made him hard to ignore. Another MP asked rebel leader John Hampden if he knew the scruffy oaf who had just spoken. Hampden, replied:

That slovenly fellow which you see before us ... will be one of the greatest men in England.

Oliver was 41 at the time, and a complete nobody. He was also a hot-head with a temper that could erupt like a volcano. In one speech Oliver was so rude towards a fellow MP that he was almost reported to the House of

Commons. Who'd have guessed that this loud-mouthed lout would become the most powerful man in all England?

The road to war

Less than two years after the Long Parliament was called the whole country was at war. How did it come to that? To start with it was a game of bluff between the king and Parliament. Both were struggling for power and neither side was willing to give an inch. No one really believed it would come to an all out fight. The king and Parliament were rather like two playground bullies sizing up to each other.

Of course what they really said to each other was a bit more serious than that. Charles was facing problems on all sides. North of the border he'd failed to put down a Scottish rebellion. That was soon followed by a particularly bloody uprising in Ireland. But it wasn't all bad.

Pym, the leader of the rebels in Parliament was quick to see the danger. To unite opposition to the king he drew up a document called 'the Grand Remonstrance'. It was the longest whinge in history. It had no less than 200 clauses, listing every gripe and grudge that Parliament held against the king for the last 16 years.

IMPRISONING M.PS... COLLECTING UNLAWFUL TAXES... WEARING A SILLY BEARD... MARRYING A FOREIGNER...

The Grand Remonstrance was MPs blowing a raspberry in the king's face. Parliament knew very well it was an insult but went ahead and did it anyway. Oliver Cromwell was naturally on the side of Parliament.

Many royalist MPs, however, thought poking their tongues out at the king was going too far. After a long and bitter debate the Grand Remonstrance was passed by just 11 votes (159 to 148). In fact it only squeezed through by a cunning trick. The rebel MPs waited until after dark to force a vote. By that time most of the old MPs had crawled into bed and the young ones had gone off to town. As soon as they saw they were in the majority the rebels cried 'Vote! Vote!' Never mind that it was one o' clock in the morning!

To Charles the Grand Remonstrance was the final straw and he tried a trick of his own. Unfortunately, the king was no good at tricks and this one backfired.

Here's how a newspaper of the time might have reported the incident.

THE CAVALIER CRYER

JANUARY 1642

KING FAILS TO GET THE BIRD

In a sensational move, the king burst in on Parliament today to arrest five of Parliament's leading rebels.

For months a showdown has been looming between the king and Parliament's ringleader, John Pym. King Pym – as Londoners call him – had recently enraged Charles by calling for Queen Henrietta Maria to be imprisoned. Charles replied by accusing Pym and four other MPs of treason. Instead of going into hiding, Pym has challenged the king to act by remaining in the House of Commons.

Pym: Stayed in the House

Barged in

The Commons was silent as Charles entered with a troop of soldiers. He scanned the rows of faces for his enemies. But they were gone. As Charles had come in the front door, Pym and his pals had escaped out the back. They were already on their way down the Thames by barge. 'I see all my birds have flown,' said the red-faced king.

All year the struggle between the king and Parliament has been smouldering. Now Charles's attempt to use force has lit the blue touch-paper. Whatever promises he makes to Parliament, he's shown he means to rule as a dictator. Barricades are going up all over London. England is on the brink of war.

Meanwhile, as all hell broke loose in London and the king fled from the capital, Oliver Cromwell was preparing to take the stage. Up to now he'd had only a bit part to play – a third spear-carrier on the side of Parliament. It was the war that handed him a lead part and most of the best lines. Oliver was about to become dead famous.

WAR IS HELL!

THE CAVALIER CRYER

22 AUGUST 1642

IT'S WAR!

It's official. After all the rumours and threats, war has been declared. This morning the king raised his standard at Nottingham. No sooner was it up than a dreadful storm blew it down again. Doom merchants are claiming that short of a plague of frogs croaking 'Death to the king!', Charles couldn't have wished for a worse omen.

Bad luck for Charles?

Nobbled navy

The country is already dividing for or against the king. He has right on his side but in some ways his position looks wobbly. Parliament holds all the main ports including London and Bristol, and the navy has also run up the flag for the rebels. Charles is probably wishing he'd never spent all those taxes on building a strong navy!

War's a bore

Many people aren't keen on a war. From Yorkshire to Cornwall, the gentry have made pacts to stay neutral and stay out of the fighting. One reluctant soldier, the Earl of Dorset even penned a poem about his feelings:

'I cannot act a soldier's part,
Nor freezing lie in trenches,
But wish myself with all my heart,
At Chelsey with my wenches.'

Earl: 'Women not war'

Whatever the dainty earl may say, it looks like everyone will have to choose sides sooner or later. Reports say fighting has already broken out. If you don't join one side for protection, the other will pinch what you own. In this war, sitting on the fence could prove uncomfortable.

The country had woken up to find it was at war. This was a bit of a shock to say the least. War against old enemies like France or Spain was nothing new, but this was a war where both sides were – damn it – English!

I SAY, CHAPS! THAT'S JUST NOT CRICKET!

Outside London, people thought the world had gone stark staring bonkers. Perhaps it had. England had survived the Norman invasion, the Spanish Armada and Henry VIII's head collection – but now it was about to tear itself apart. People were being asked to choose between royalist and Roundhead. Civil War had broken out, and most people doubted that it would be very civil at all.

Cool Cavaliers and rude Roundheads

The two enemy sides in the war were known as Cavaliers and Roundheads. Today we think of Cavaliers as dashing and devil-may-care but in fact both names were originally insults. The names were yelled back and forth during the riots in London. 'Roundheads' was aimed at the London apprentices, a mob of lads who wore cropped hair, scorning the 'love-locks' worn by Cavaliers. The name 'Cavalier' came from 'cabaleros' – hated Spanish soldiers who were enemies of Protestants. A Puritan pamphlet of the time mentions:

> …*that Legion of Devils, that heap of scum and drosse and garbage of the land, made up of Jesuits and Papists and Atheists, that bloody and butcherly Generation commonly knowne by the names of Cavaliers.*

So we can safely say that 'Cavalier' wasn't a compliment.

The richer Cavaliers could usually be recognized by their fashion taste. They loved to cut a dash in lace, ribbons and rustling silks.

Rudely dressed Roundheads, on the other hand, were often fashion disasters. Strict Puritans believed that plain clothes showed a humble heart.

Cromwell himself wore his hair long but, asked to choose between scarlet satin and dull leather, there was no contest.

LIGHT OR MUD BROWN, SIR?

Oddly enough, both dashing Cavaliers and rude Roundheads smelled equally bad under their clothes. It's unlikely that anyone took any notice when a French writer in 1640 suggested:

An occasional bath should be taken, the hands washed daily and the face every day or so.

Even the rich and wealthy thought baths were a waste of time. (The poor didn't have any water so they just wore their filth like a second skin.) Lice were common and handkerchiefs were rarely used for blowing noses. So what were they for? To look fashionable of course!

Picking sides

Despite their fashion tastes, it wasn't always so easy to tell who was a Roundhead or Cavalier. Not all royalists dressed like princes and not all Roundheads were seriously dull Puritans. To make matters even more confusing there was no such thing as army uniform at the start of the Civil War. In the heat of battle, often your only chance of recognizing your enemy was by the colour of his sash or armband. No doubt this led to a few unfortunate accidents.

The quarrel between king and Parliament split the country down the middle. Roughly speaking the north and the west (including Wales) were for the king while the south and the east were cheering for Parliament. The Midlands, as you can see, had trouble making up its mind.

The war has often been depicted as a class struggle between the toffee-nosed Cavaliers and the common-as-muck Roundheads. The real picture was much more complicated. Although most of the House of Lords fought for the king, some nobles and plenty of gentlemen turned out for Parliament.

In fact, religion played a bigger part in deciding which side to join. Most Anglicans and Catholics backed the king, while most Puritans lined up for Parliament.

Choosing sides wasn't always easy. The war divided families and friends. Many didn't even believe in the cause they were fighting for. Sir Edmund Verney joined the royalists even though he thought the king was wrong to fight.

I have eaten his bread and served him for thirty years and will not do so base a thing as to forsake him; and rather choose to lose my life, which I am sure I shall do.

Sadly for Verney he turned out to be dead right. A few months later he was killed defending the king's standard at the battle of Edgehill. Poor Verney was one of many who entered the war with a heavy heart.

Oliver Cromwell had few such doubts.

Oliver's Secret Diary   29th August 1642

War at last! About time! I'm sick of all this waiting.

Today I went to Huntingdon to start recruiting. I spoke plain with them. My commission says we're fighting for 'King and Parliament'. What a pile of horse-dung! Everyone knows we're fighting against the king. I told the townsfolk: 'If the king happens to be in the ranks of the army I'm charging, I'll shoot him dead like any other man.' If they couldn't do the same they shouldn't sign up with me.

I fancy this blunt speaking won many hearts. Too bad if it didn't! I don't want any dithering milksops in my army!

Oliver saw the war as a fight for religious freedom.

> *Religion was not the thing at first contested for, but God brought it to that issue at the last.*

A cracking war

Unlike boring European wars, the Civil War was fought at a fast and furious pace. In Germany they'd had the yawning Thirty Years War while Spain and the Netherlands had been fighting for eighty years! The English thought that was boring. If they were going to fight they reckoned they might as well get on with it.

This wasn't good news for everyone. Many professional soldiers travelled to England hoping the war might pay their wages for the next twenty years! In fact the war was pretty well over in less than six. In that short space of time there was no shortage of action. There were more battles, sieges and skirmishes than most soldiers saw in a lifetime.

> *'Twas the general Maxim in this War, Where is the Enemy? Let us go and fight them.*

Daniel Defoe (author of *Robinson Crusoe*)

At the start of the war the two sides were fairly evenly matched. What decided the result was the skill of the leaders on each side. Let's meet some of the key players.

53

Prince Rupert of the Rhine

Nickname: The Mad Cavalier.

Claim to fame: King Charles's Dutch nephew and commander of the king's cavalry.

Personality: Young, brave, dashing, brilliant – no wonder Charles's other commanders didn't like him.

Tactics: Rupert liked his cavalry to charge straight into the enemy, firing their pistols and then drawing their swords. It wasn't a wise move to stand in his way.

Weakness: His cavalry charges were like a runaway train – they just kept on going!

Odd fact: Rupert had a pet spaniel called Boy. Boy was trained to jump in the air at the word 'Charles' or cock his leg if his master said 'Pym' (the rebel MP).

Lord Digby

Claim to fame: Royalist general and close chum of Charles.

Personality: Hopeless optimist. Late in the war,

encouraged Charles to believe he could win even when all England knew he was beaten.

Motto: It's a lovely day tomorrow.

Big mistake: Squabbling with Prince Rupert. They couldn't stand each other.

Odd fact: Only soldier to fight for the English, French and Spanish armies. Digby would fight for anyone who was silly enough to have him.

William Cavendish, Earl of Newcastle

Claim to fame: Commander of the Royalist forces in the north.

Personality: Stout Yorkshireman.

Motto: Never run away.

Big mistake: Never running away.

Odd fact: His army were called Whitecoats because of their easy to spot white uniforms. Nearly all of them perished at the battle of Marston Moor, refusing to surrender.

Earl of Essex

Position: Commander of the Parliament's army at start of the war.

Personality: Solid, pipe-smoking, loyal and pretty useless really.

Motto: Ready to die.

Big mistake: In 1644 Essex disobeyed orders and marched into the south-west where he got cut off and lost his entire army. Well anyone can make a mistake.

Odd fact: When the gloomy earl set off to war he took his coffin with him just in case.

Sir Thomas Fairfax

Nickname: Black Tom, because of his long dark hair and black eyes. (Not because he was a cat.)

Claim to fame: Commander-in-Chief of Parliament's New Model Army.

Personality: Quiet, modest, religious – except when he got into battle and became a wild dangerous maniac.

Odd fact: Lady Fairfax accompanied her hubby to war and was no shrinking violet herself. Once she was captured by the enemy but they sent her straight back in a coach.

Oliver Cromwell

Nickname: Ironsides – given to him and his soldiers by his rival, Prince Rupert.

Claim to fame: Started the war as a nobody but rose to be Parliament's biggest hero.

Personality: Bold, determined, never-beaten commander.

Motto: Charge!

Odd fact: Two of Oliver's sons, Oliver and Henry, marched to war in the same army, following in their dad's footsteps. Sadly Oliver junior bit the dust.

WARTS AND ALL ~ ROTTEN WARFARE

War in Cromwell's day was a very different business to modern warfare. Although most Englishmen had no experience of fighting, they still had strong ideas about tactics. Cromwell was one of the first to see the need for a trained, disciplined army. At the start the armies drew up in definite formations opposite each other. Once the battle got under way, however, it often became a free for all, where no one had a clue who was winning.

If you joined the army in the Civil War, you'd be put into one of four sections. Some were more dangerous than others.

1 PIKEMEN
- Wooden spears almost five metres long
- Helmet and armour on chest, backs and thighs

SURVIVAL CHANCES: 5/10 Vulnerable on foot but you can make your point with that pike.

2 CAVALRY
- Horse (essential to joining the cavalry)
- Heavy armour
- Sword for hand-to-hand fighting
- Pistols – can only fire one shot each (so don't miss!)

SURVIVAL CHANCES: 8/10 The cavalry charge is the key weapon in battle so you'll be in the thick of it. But at least on a horse you can get away quickly!

3 DRAGOONS
- Soldiers on horseback
- Armed with guns called carbines

SURVIVAL CHANCES: 7/10 Much the same as the cavalry except that aiming a gun on horseback is like trying to thread a needle on a rollercoaster.

4 MUSKETEERS
- Long heavy musket with a rest (to use when firing)
- Bandolier (shoulder belt)
- Twists of paper holding gunpowder
- Helmet but little armour

SURVIVAL CHANCES: 4/10 Those muskets are a soldier's nightmare. Once they're fired they take an age to reload.

At the start of the war the cavalry were usually gentry or aristocrats. (They were the only ones who owned horses.) Oliver himself would have grown up riding horses on his father's farm in Huntingdon. Any noble was expected to be a master of horsemanship. King Charles, too, would have got a sore bottom from hours spent in the saddle.

The cavalry charge was the deadliest weapon in the war. Imagine standing your ground while hundreds of horsemen thunder towards you, packed closely together and firing their pistols. Cavalry were hard to control in the din of battle however. To charge the enemy once was one thing, to turn and charge again was quite another. Usually it was chaos after the first attack.

Battles were surprisingly small affairs. There were never more than 20,000 men involved – less than half the number that watch Manchester United live on a Saturday. The outcome of a battle was often decided by the quick thinking of the commanders. Here's how a general might have described his team formation before the big game.

Biscuits, bed and breakfast

Whether you were riding in the cavalry or lugging a heavy musket, war was a rotten business. Cannons and ammunition had to be dragged for miles over foul muddy roads in freezing winter weather. To eat you got the princely daily ration of:

ONE POUND OF BISCUIT, ONE POUND OF CHEESE PER PERSON.

A pound is a hefty portion (2.2 kilograms) but you'd soon get sick of mouldy cheese and dry biscuits after a few weeks. Even worse, armies sometimes ran out food altogether. When Edmund Ludlow fought for Parliament in the battle of Edgehill he hadn't eaten for days. Not only was his stomach rumbling, he was so frozen in his heavy armour that he had to walk up and down all night to keep warm. When Ludlow did finally get some meat, his jaws were too frozen to chew anything!

Another nobleman, Sir Adrian Scrope, found himself left for dead after a battle. Wounded and stark naked he was in real danger of freezing to death. About midnight, to keep himself warm, he crawled underneath the only warmth he could find – a dead body!

There were rarely tents to sleep in. Armies adopted a practice called 'freequarter'. This was rotten for soldiers but even worse for villagers. When an army arrived in a village, the officer would knock on doors and announce to the lucky owners that they'd been chosen to offer bed and breakfast. This wasn't a request. The soldiers simply marched in and made themselves at home. In return the villagers were given vouchers by the army. You can imagine how thrilled they were!

Freequarter was bad enough but victorious armies could be even worse. If your town was stormed by the enemy, it was safest to leave quickly. Generals often found it impossible to control their troops, so they let them run wild in the town. As an example, here's just a taste of what Prince Rupert's soldiers got up to in Birmingham:

> ...they ran into every house cursing and damning, threatening and terrifying the poor women most terribly, setting naked swords and pistols to their breasts... That night few or none of them went to bed but sat up revelling, robbing and tyrannizing over the poor affrighted women and prisoners ... drinking drunk healths to Prince Rupert's dog.

It was certainly a dog's life being a civilian during the Civil War.

On the up

What about Oliver Cromwell himself? He certainly didn't think that war was rotten. While others agonized over whether the war was a good idea, Cromwell had no such doubts. He was fighting for the right of Parliament to govern and the right to worship any way he liked. After all, if Puritans wanted to be dull and gloomy why shouldn't they be allowed to get on with it?

The war was the making of Cromwell. At the start he was a 43-year-old MP whom nobody had ever heard of. By the end he'd become Oliver Ironsides – a military genius up there in history with Julius Caesar, Napoleon and the Duke of Wellington. Yet, amazingly, he'd never been a soldier in his life. So how did he do it?

TIMELINE:
OLIVER AND HIS IRONSIDES

1642: CIVIL WAR KICKS OFF. KING RAISES STANDARD AT NOTTINGHAM.

SOMEONE'S GOT TO RAISE STANDARDS ROUND HERE!

BATTLE OF EDGEHILL— BOTH SIDES CLAIM VICTORY.

RESULT!

1643: COLONEL CROMWELL JOINS THE EASTERN ASSOCIATION ARMY. SIEGE OF GLOUCESTER. SCOTS ENTER THE WAR AGAINST THE KING.

CAN WE PLAY?

1644: CROMWELL PROMOTED TO LIEUTENANT GENERAL. DEFEATS DASHING PRINCE RUPERT AT BATTLE OF MARSTON MOOR. CREATES NEW MODEL ARMY.

AND THE ENEMY WILL THINK THEY'RE REAL!

1645: ROYALISTS GET ANOTHER PASTING AT THE BATTLE OF NASEBY.

IT'S A RIGHT ROYAL DISASTER!

1646: CHARLES THROWS IN THE TOWEL. CURTAIN DOWN ON THE FIRST CIVIL WAR.

COMING SOON:
CIVIL WAR 2

1647: PASS THE CHARLIE: CHARLES HANDS HIMSELF OVER TO THE SCOTS. SCOTS HAND CHARLES BACK TO PARLIAMENT. ARMY KIDNAPS THE KING. CHARLES ESCAPES TO THE ISLE OF WIGHT.

I'M THE KING OF THE CASTLE.

1648: SECOND CIVIL WAR. CROMWELL SWATS THE SCOTS, WHO ARE NOW FIGHTING FOR CHARLIE, AT THE BATTLE OF PRESTON.

IT WAS MORE FUN WHEN WE WERE ON THE OTHER SIDE!

1649: CHARLES GETS THE CHOP. ENGLAND IS DECLARED A COMMONWEALTH.

I DECLARE THIS COMMONWEALTH OPEN!

OLIVER AND THE NOT-SO-CIVIL WAR

Cromwell started the war as a mere captain. Parliament's army was led by Lord General Essex (the carry-your-own-coffin earl). Cromwell was in the cavalry but he was only a humble captain and hard to spot.

SPOT THE OLIVER

TROOP NO. 67

No one paid Oliver much attention but that would soon change once the fighting started. Charles meanwhile had left Nottingham and was planning to attack the capital. Essex's army marched north intending to cut him off. For a while the two armies blundered around without finding each other. Then Charles decided to stand and fight. The first big battle of the war was at Edgehill, near Banbury, in Oxfordshire.

Here is the news

Early in the war both sides saw the importance of news reports. It was simple: if you kept telling people you were winning, they might start to believe you. Obviously it wasn't possible to watch the telly to find out how the war was going, so both sides started their own newspapers. The royalist version was called *Mercurius Aulicus* – while its Roundhead rival went under the equally thrilling title of *Special Passages*.

In the propaganda battle, it was the royalists who grabbed the headlines. Their newspaper appeared every week, usually on a Monday and was read by both sides because it was the best source of information. Accurate it may have been, but it was bound to be just a teeny bit biased. Here's how a royal rag might have reported on Edgehill.

THE CAVALIER CRYER

22 AUGUST 1642

KING SMASHES ROUNDHEAD RABBLE

First blood in the Civil War has gone to brave King Charles. The two sides met at Edgehill today at 3 o'clock in the afternoon and the battle raged until nightfall. Both sides are claiming victory but the king denies the Roundhead view on the grounds that he's always right.

Despite the fact that he has absolutely no experience of war Charles has decided to take personal command of his forces. Such bravery is typical of our noble king!

King Charles – new to war

Admittedly his leaders got off on the wrong foot by quarrelling over the battle plan. When Charles took his nephew Rupert's advice, the veteran Earl of Lindsey stormed off in a sulk. 'I'm not being lectured by a young pup like him,' said livid Lindsey.

It was daring Prince Rupert who caught the eye however. The Prince's cavalry swept downhill on the Roundheads below and scattered them like pigeons. Then Rupert's horsemen thundered on … and on, leaving the battlefield far behind.

Seeing them go, Parliament's infantry launched a counter-attack and for a moment the king's life looked in danger. Luckily, dashing Rupert dashed back to save the day.

Haunting

After today's battle local shepherds claimed they saw ghostly horsemen in the sky re-enacting the conflict. 'We heard drums and trumpets and awful groans like men was a-dying,' said one. 'It made the wool stand up on the back of my sheep.'

Sheep – went baarmy

It is surely an omen that the evil rebellion against the king is doomed. Death to the rebels and long live His Majesty!

This royally biased tale doesn't quite paint the full picture. The fact was that at Edgehill the royalists blew their chance of kicking off with a win. Charles blundered by taking command of his army, since he hadn't the faintest clue how to fight a battle. Despite this, Rupert's charge could have won the day but he blew it by galloping off, caught up in the heat of the chase. Parliament then fought back to claim a draw.

Charles could still have grabbed the advantage if he'd pressed on to reach London. Instead he dithered and was turned back by a rabble of Londoners wielding sticks and pitchforks. The king was a master at snatching defeat from the jaws of victory.

The history of the Civil War is littered with boobs and blunders. Surrounded by amateurs, someone with sense and determination was bound to become a hero. So where was Oliver Cromwell? His enemies later claimed he was too cowardly even to show up at Edgehill. One daft royalist story claims Oliver climbed a church steeple to avoid the battle and swung around a bell rope. Maybe Oliver penned his own version of events in his diary.

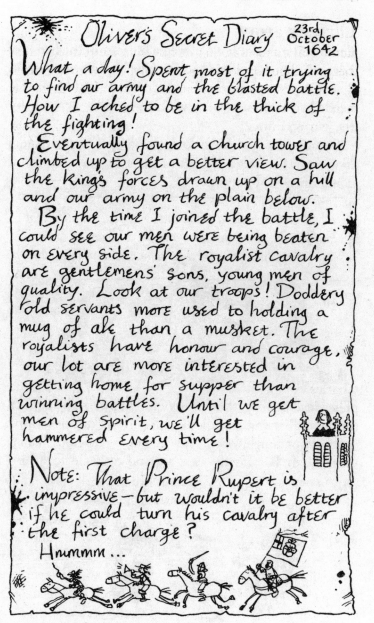

Oliver's Secret Diary
23rd October 1642

What a day! Spent most of it trying to find our army and the blasted battle. How I ached to be in the thick of the fighting!

Eventually found a church tower and climbed up to get a better view. Saw the king's forces drawn up on a hill and our army on the plain below.

By the time I joined the battle, I could see our men were being beaten on every side. The royalist cavalry are gentlemens' sons, young men of quality. Look at our troops! Doddery old servants more used to holding a mug of ale than a musket. The royalists have honour and courage, our lot are more interested in getting home for supper than winning battles. Until we get men of spirit, we'll get hammered every time!

Note: That Prince Rupert is impressive — but wouldn't it be better if he could turn his cavalry after the first charge?

Hmmmm...

71

Oliver's army

Cromwell may not have played a big part in the battle of Edgehill, but he learned some valuable lessons from it. The memory of Rupert's charge stuck with him. He needed to build a cavalry which would be a match for the pin-up Prince.

Cromwell could have looked for sons of gentlemen like Rupert. Instead he went out of his way to recruit commoners and poor men.

> *I had rather have a plain russet-coated captain that knows what he fights for, and loves what he knows, than that which you call a gentleman and nothing else.*

The real quality that Colonel Cromwell (he'd been promoted by the way) looked for in his recruits wasn't nobility or toughness, it was … um … religion! It may sound daft but loving God was no obstacle to killing your enemy.

72

Remember, Cromwell was a devout Puritan. Puritans were disciplined and godly; they didn't fight, mutiny, drink or steal – which was the normal routine for an army in those days. By May 1643 Cromwell had recruited 2,000 disciplined and godly soldiers. He called them 'his lovely company'. Royalists, no doubt, called them other names.

Three cheers for the king

Despite Cromwell's progress, the summer of 1643 didn't go well for Parliament. The headlines in the royalist paper must have made gloomy reading for Oliver.

It was bad luck for King Charles that even his successes backfired. At this point the Scots decided to join the war, but not on the king's side. Worried about rumours that the king was talking to Irish Catholics, the Scots joined Parliament. And there was more bad news to come for the king. The following year he suffered a major defeat.

THE CAVALIER CRYER

2 JULY 1644

MOOR WOE FOR CHARLES

Marston Moor, North Yorkshire. Royal forces today suffered a crushing defeat here by the combined forces of the Scots and Parliament. The battle has left the king's power in the north in tatters.

Things had all started so well when Prince Rupert relieved the city of York from the besieging Scots. The Marquis of Newcastle had hailed Rupert as the saviour of the north. His tune soon changed when Rupert ordered him to meet at dawn next morning to attack the enemy. The miffed marquis failed to show up on time.

Newcastle: Better things to do
By the time the royal forces were ready, any chance of surprise was lost.

Cheat trick

With little daylight left, Rupert decided there would be no battle that day. As the Prince dismissed his troops, Cromwell played a dirty trick by launching an attack. Eyewitnesses say the royalists might have held if Lord Byron, on the left flank, hadn't lost his nerve and charged against orders. Byron's cavalry got bogged down in the mud and Cromwell's men cut through them like butter. Showing remarkable skill (for a Roundhead) Cromwell then swept round the back of Rupert's army and attacked the other flank.

There's no doubt that the might of Cromwell's cavalry won the day. It is the first time that Rupert has been beaten and afterwards he gave Cromwell's men the nickname 'Ironsides'.

Cromwell – star turn
It seems Parliament have a rising star in their ranks. (Though our readers say he's not half as handsome as dashing Rupert.)

75

Moaning Manchester

Cromwell wasn't just a pretty face – actually he wasn't a pretty face at all – but he was pretty clever. At this point in the war he grasped that Parliament's army needed total reorganization. The soldiers were sick and starving while most civilians were sick and tired of having them in their houses. Not only this, Cromwell reckoned that some of Parliament's generals weren't up to the job. A big row was brewing between Cromwell and his commander, the Earl of Manchester. Manchester was horrified that Cromwell was making officers out of footmen and cart-drivers.

I SAY! YOU CHAPS, YOU JUST AREN'T GENTLEMEN!

A horrible truth was beginning to dawn on the earl. If the king got the chop after the war, then wealthy lords like him might also lose their power. Manchester also moaned:

> *If we fight* (the king) *a hundred times and beat him ninety times he will be king still. But if he beat us but once, or the last time, we shall be hanged, we shall lose our estates and our posterities be undone.*

You can imagine iron Oliver's reply to that kind of cowardly drivel.

Oliver's Secret Diary 23rd November 1644

That Manchester is a moaning minnie! He's scared of losing the war and he's just as scared of winning it. So what in heaven was the point of starting it in the first place!

The weakling will have to go and I've thought of a brilliant plan to get rid of him. We'll pass a law in Parliament that says no member of the House of Lords or Commons can hold an army command. That'll mean Manchester and his toffee-nosed chums will have to resign. Then we can get on with building an army to win the war.

There's one slight snag. I'm an MP myself, which means I'd have to resign too. But would it come to that? Everyone knows who's the best cavalry commander on our side – and probably in the land. Can Parliament do without him? Modesty forbids me to say more... (clue: his initials are O.C.)

As usual Cromwell was right. The new law – the Self Denying Ordinance – was passed and Manchester was out on his lordly ear. Then Parliament set about building a new improved force called the New Model Army.

Cromwell, of course, was heavily involved in the plans. Sir Thomas Fairfax – who wasn't an MP – was appointed General-in-Chief. But one vacancy still remained. Who should lead the cavalry and be second in command?

The New Model Army would not only win the war for Parliament – it would also shape the peace afterwards. Most local armies were anxious to get home after a tough day on the battlefield. The New Model Army was different. It was a national army paid to fight wherever it was needed.

On the royalist side Prince Rupert wasn't so lucky. He had no control over the king's barmy armies in the west and north. Timid Charles gave all his commanders the freedom to do as they liked. This meant that poor Rupert was only a paper commander. He never knew whether the other generals would obey his orders and turn up for the battle or not.

Wild women

There's no doubt that Oliver was the star of the war. If there'd been a 'War Hero of the Year' award he would have won it hands down. Yet there were other heroes whose tales were less well known. Heroines too. In fact many of the women were more than a match for the men.

The petticoat private

Those who fought in the cavalry at Marston Moor may remember a Yorkshireman called Ingleby. At least they thought he was a Yorkshireman. In fact, Private Ingleby was a she! Jane Ingleby, the daughter of a Yorkshireman yeoman, fought in the battle and was believed to have escaped home wounded. She inspired a popular ballad of the time:

> *Her husband was a soldier and to the wars did go,*
> *And she would be his comrade, the truth of all is so,*
> *She put on men's apparel and bore him company,*
> *As many in the army for truth can testify.*

Queen Henrietta Maria

Charles's wife, Queen Henrietta Maria, didn't plan to sit quietly on the sidelines. She fled abroad at the outbreak of the war with the crown jewels in her handbag. Her aim was to raise money and buy arms for her husband's army.

By 1643 she was back in England, calling herself the 'She-Majesty Generalissima over all'. Henrietta marched around the countryside with an escort of 5,000 soldiers, rallying support for her husband. The following year Her She-Majesty was at  Exeter where the city was under siege by the pipe-smoking Earl of Essex and his Roundheads. Henrietta was about to give birth and was sure that she was about to die. After the birth she lost all feeling in one arm and the sight in one eye. Accompanied by a priest and a doctor, she escaped from Exeter and eventually fled to France. Charles arrived at the city two weeks after his wife had gone. She never saw him alive again.

Battling Lady Bankes

Lady Mary Bankes's husband was away fighting with the king when Corfe Castle was besieged. But no Roundhead was going to rob her without a fight. When Sir William Erle and his troops attacked the castle, Lady Mary fought back. Her only 'army' was her daughters, some serving women and five soldiers. Despite their superior numbers, the besiegers were unable to take the castle. When news came that the king was not far off, they fled and left Lady Bankes the victor.

Sadly, after hanging on to her castle for two years, her downfall came about because of the treachery of a lily-livered man. One of her lieutenants, a wimp called Pitman, let the enemy on to the castle walls because he was fed up with eating measly siege rations. The troops rushed the defences, Corfe was taken and Lady Bankes' private war was over. (But pity Pitman if his mistress ever got her hands on him.)

Brilliant Brilliana

Other Cavalier women were not to be outdone. Lady Brilliana Harley defended Brampton Bryan during a seven-week assault by the Roundheads. An eyewitness account shows she wasn't the only woman to put herself in the firing line.

Upon the seventh (of August) in the afternoon ... (the enemy) planted another great gun against the west part of our castle. The third shot the bullet came in at a window, shaved the walls, which hurt the Lady Colburn, and struck out one of her eyes. Lieutenant-Colonel Wright's wife was hurt, but neither of them mortally...

Upon the 9th the enemy planted five great guns, as if they meant this day to have beaten it to dust... The noble lady (Brilliana) was ... more courageous than ever.

Brave Brilliana saw off the enemy and held on to Brampton Bryan. Sadly when her home was again besieged, it's said she died of exhaustion.

The Cavaliers claimed most of the war's heroines but not most of the victories. In 1645 the last major battle of the first Civil War was fought. It was the first test of Cromwell's New Model Army and they didn't let themselves down. The battle was fought in the Midlands at a village called Naseby.

THE CAVALIER CRYER

14 JUNE 1645

IT'S IRONSIDES AGAIN!

Royalist forces were swept from the field yesterday in what may be the last big battle of the war. Once again the name of Oliver Cromwell is being toasted by Roundheads as the hero of the hour. It's said when he arrived in camp the cry went up: 'Ironsides is come!'

The line-up

The battle followed a familiar pattern, with Rupert sweeping through on the Roundheads' left and putting them to flight. It was all going the king's way but yet again, Rupert's cavalry lost their heads and galloped on a mile. By the time the king's nephew got back, his side had lost the battle.

Backwards march

While Rupert rode off, Cromwell broke the royalist left and turned on their hard-pressed infantry in the centre. At this point, the king tried to intervene. He appeared to urge his horse forward to lead his reserve army to the rescue. It might have worked too, if a courtier hadn't grabbed the

Charles – wrong turn

bridle of Charles's horse to stop him from riding into danger. Seeing the king turn, his men thought he was beating a retreat and followed gladly.

Left to face Cromwell alone, the infantry surrendered and the battle was soon over. Yet again rotten luck has cost the king victory.

Hands up if you surrender

End game

Critics are saying that the game is up for the king. Only Bristol remains in royalist hands. Rupert has advised him to ask for peace terms, but Charles refuses to admit defeat. Yesterday he said defiantly: 'I may have lost a battle but I haven't lost the war.'

ACTUALLY, YOU'VE LOST BOTH!

Body count

Charles found himself cornered at Oxford, while Cromwell and Fairfax mopped up the remains of his supporters in the south. In a short time the war was over.

The two sides had lined up with fairly equal armies at the beginning, but how had they fared by the end? Have a look at the chart below. It shows that less than half the deaths actually happened in battle.

DIED IN BATTLE	34,000 PARLIAMENT 51,000 ROYALIST
DEADLY DISEASE	100,000 BOTH SIDES COMBINED
ACCIDENTAL DEATH (CHAAAARGE!!!) SPLAT	300 BOTH SIDES COMBINED
TOTAL CIVIL WAR DEATHS	185,300
TAKEN PRISONER	34,000 PARLIAMENT 83,000 ROYALIST

The Civil War may have been a triumph for Oliver, but it was a disaster for the country. Not many people know this, but a higher *percentage* of the population died in the Civil War than in either the First or Second World Wars!

During the war the country went to ruin. Taxes were crippling and many churches and stately homes were damaged or burnt to the ground. The atmosphere of religious enthusiasm also gave rise to some weird events. No one had a weirder career than Matthew Hopkins.

WARTS AND ALL ~ HOW TO SPOT A WITCH.

Hopkins's career as a witchfinder began in 1644, near the end of the war. In March he stumbled across a company of witches who met every Friday night to offer sacrifices to the devil. Hopkins's evidence saw twenty of them hanged. According to him, four of them had sent the devil in the shape of a bear to kill him.

Encouraged by this early success, Hopkins set up as a 'Witchfinder General' and travelled around the country unmasking witches. As it turned out England was crawling with them. Not that Hopkins's services came free of course: he charged 20 shillings for every town he visited. Anyone suspected of witchcraft was urged to confess – and then hanged. A number of 'signs' were supposed to prove his victims were witches. Here are some of his favourites:

1 Look for three 'paps' (breasts) – the sure mark of a witch.

2 Tie the witch to a table in a locked room for two days without food or sleep. Leave a hole in the door for her 'imps' (devils) to come in through. Then walk her about till her feet blister. The witch is sure to confess!

3 Throw her in a pool with her thumbs and toes bound together. If she sinks, she's innocent (but probably drowned). If she 'swims' it proves she's a witch and must be hanged.

It's no wonder Hopkins got so many confessions from his victims. Who wouldn't confess after being chucked in a lake or tied to a table for two days! One old, one-legged beggar woman confessed to keeping 'imps' called 'Black rabbit', 'Sugar', 'Polecat' and 'Vinegar Tom' – apparently this last was a greyhound with an ox's head and horns. Another woman's imp turned out to be nothing more devilish than a hen.

Not everyone was fooled by the Witchfinder General. John Gaul – a Puritan vicar and a Cromwellian – claimed Hopkins was a rotten fake.

> *Every old woman with a wrinkled face, a hairy lip, a squeaking voice, or a scolding tongue, having a spindle in her hand, and a dog and a cat by her side is not only suspected but pronounced for a witch.*

The real witch in Gaul's opinion was Matthew Hopkins.

One tale says that Hopkins was eventually tried for witchcraft himself. And, fittingly one of his own 'signs' was used to test his guilt. His hands and feet were tied together and he was thrown into a pool. Hopkins was lucky that he 'swam' – but not that lucky. According to his own test he'd just proved he was a witch and the court ordered him to be hanged. That spelt the end for the Witchfinder General.

I DEMAND A RETRIAL!

The sneaky Stuart

Witchy Hopkins wasn't the only one in a tight spot after the war. It looked like the end of the line for King Charles I. He'd gambled everything on winning the war and lost. Now he'd have to eat the humble pie that Parliament had prepared for him. Or would he? Sneaky

Charles was a disaster as a general but he still had a few tricks up his sleeve.

Charles still believed he was born to be king so no one could take away his throne. He was prepared to do anything to regain power – and if that meant lying and switching sides, he'd do it. Perhaps if he'd kept a secret diary himself it would have revealed the game he was playing.

Charles I's Secret Diary

5th May 1646

Ha ha! Sneaked out of Oxford in disguise and got away. Those Roundheads are no match for a man of my intelligence! I cut my long, flowing locks short, dressed in dark clothes and wore a false beard. I looked for all the world like a servant. Me – the king of England – what a jest! It was all I could do to stop myself laughing out loud as we sneaked past the guard.

Arrived tonight in Southwell near Nottingham.

ME IN CUNNING DISGUISE

1st June

Have handed myself over to the Scots and thrown myself on their mercy.

I know the sneaky Scots fought against me in the War, but they're a safer bet than Warty Cromwell and his ugly Roundheads. I'll pretend to be interested in the Scots' dreadful Presbyterian religion. Maybe they'll lend me their army for a year or two. There's life in the old dog yet!

20 December

Have been here seven long months now. Every day long-faced Scottish clerics come to lecture me on converting to Presbyterianism. I pretend to listen, while I work out the next move in my game of chess. (I'm 99 games to 3 in the lead against my chaplain!) It's only chess that keeps me sane.

By the way, Parliament offered me peace terms but I turned them down flat. No one gets the King in checkmate that easily!

ha ha!

Charles wasn't only playing chess, he was playing for time. He knew that divisions had started to appear in his enemies' ranks. It was only a matter of time before they started fighting each other. A fierce struggle for power had begun, with the king used as the football between the two sides. Charles, as usual, imagined he was the key player, but that turned out to be Oliver Cromwell.

OLIVER AND CHOPPING CHARLIE

At the end of the Civil War, a beaten royalist called Sir Jacob Astley surrendered to the Roundheads with the words:

> *You have done your work now, you may go and play, unless you will fall out among yourselves.*

Astley's prediction was dead right. While the war was being fought the different groups on Parliament's side worked together. As soon as peace broke out, they began to behave like naughty children, squabbling over the biggest slice of cake. Who were the different groups fighting to win the peace?

1 THE ARMY
Won the war for Parliament but now getting shirty because they haven't been paid.

2 INDEPENDENTS

Want strict limits on the king's powers and no national church. Think each congregation should worship the way they want.

3 PRESBYTERIANS

In favour of minor reductions in the king's power and a national Presbyterian church like the Scots' model.

4 LEVELLERS

Radical group who want to change society completely so that even the stinking poor have a say.

Even the divisions mentioned above hid groups within groups. Cromwell, for instance, was an Independent in Parliament, but the root of his power lay in the army. The Levellers also had strong support among soldiers, while the Presbyterians were the strongest group in Parliament.

If this all sounds confusing, don't worry – even people in 1646 were confused. Those on Parliament's side had fought to stop Charles ruling as he liked. The problem was that having won the war, no one could agree how to run the country.

The most extreme ideas were put forward by the Levellers.

WARTS AND ALL ~ THE LEVELLERS

The Levellers were a religious group who wanted to 'level' society so that all were equal. Top of their list was giving the vote to everyone (except women of course – they'd have to wait another 300 years!). As one army colonel put it:

> *I think the poorest he that is in England hath a life to live as the greatest he… Every man that is to live under a government ought first by his own consent to put himself under that government (by voting for it).*

Today most people would agree, but in Cromwell's day the Levellers' demands were considered dangerous. The notion of button-makers having the same right to vote as lords and gentlemen seemed as crackpot as men walking on the moon. Cromwell thought it would lead to the whole breakdown of society. 'Break them or they will break you,' was his attitude to the Levellers. John Lilburne, the Levellers' leader, was imprisoned first by Charles I and then by Cromwell.

IT'S THE ONE THING WE AGREE UPON!

92

For one person the situation was shaping up rather nicely – Charles himself. His game-plan was to talk to everybody and agree to nothing. In that way he could stir up the maximum amount of trouble. When his enemies had finished fighting among themselves, Charles believed everyone would be glad to have their old king back. As usual, he got it hopelessly wrong. He had reckoned without the rise of Cromwell and the power of the army. In the end the king's endless haggling and playing games would lead to the chopping block.

Pass the king

By February 1647 the Scots were fed up with baby-sitting the king. They realized that he was never going to give up his Anglican faith and handed him over to the English. In return, Parliament paid up what they owed the Scots' army. (Charles teased the Scots for accepting a trifling £400,000.)

93

As Charles was escorted towards London his hopes soared anew. Church bells rang and the roads were lined with cheering subjects crying 'God save the king!'. Men and women suffering from a nasty disease called scrofula came out to touch the king, believing they'd be cured.

Even Charles's old enemy – Sir Thomas Fairfax – turned out at Nottingham to kiss the royal hand. Charles knew his subjects were sick of war, high taxes and Parliament's squabbles. He thought he only needed to wait and everything would go back to how it was in the old days.

By now the quarrel between Parliament and the army had reached a crisis. Parliament had ordered the army to disband but the soldiers mutinied. Who should they send to calm them down? Who better than Oliver Cromwell, the great war hero? Unfortunately for Parliament this backfired. Far from sending the army packing – Cromwell joined them! Oliver claimed he did it to stop the situation getting out of hand. But his sympathies lay more with the army than with Parliament. And he knew an army at his back would put him in a strong position.

Alarmed at the way things were going – Parliament made plans to grab the king. They were too late. At the end of May, an officer called Cornet Joyce kidnapped the king and took him to Newmarket under army control. Was Cromwell behind the kidnap? Again, he always denied it – but he didn't punish Joyce either.

The king was taken to Hampton Court in London. By this time the army had lost patience with Parliament and had pretty well taken over. They spent a lot of time arguing over what they should do next. These arguments were known as the Putney Debates. Oliver, as usual, had a word or two to say himself…

While Oliver sided with the moderates, the Levellers wanted to kick out Charles altogether and give the vote to every Tom, Dick and Harry.

In the end it was Charles himself who put a stop to all the hot air – by escaping once again. He was fast becoming the Houdini king. But his disappearing act played right into Cromwell's hands.

Oliver's Secret Diary

11 November 1647
Hampton Court

The King has slipped through our fingers again! It's like trying to hold on to an eel!

He vanished at suppertime, leaving only his cloak and a brief note. He claimed he's retired to 'help' the peace talks. Help, my foot! He'd start a war tomorrow if he thought he could win.

24 November

What luck! The King has turned up on the Isle of Wight. The governor there is a fine fellow. In fact he happens to be a relative of mine. Charles is now safely under lock and key in Carisbrooke Castle. He picked the wrong island for an escape. As far as I'm concerned he can stew in his prison while we keep an eye on him.

3 DECEMBER.

Waited last night outside the inn, disguised as a soldier. (Cunning, eh?) When the messenger arrived we seized the saddle bag and ripped it open. Sure enough, Charles's letter was inside. Just as I thought — the traitor is plotting with the Scots again. He's making them all sorts of promises if they'll invade England.

Much cheered by this news. Now Parliament will be forced to give up negotiations with the King. Only the army can save England from the royalist plot, but who should lead the army? It's another tricky one and no mistake...

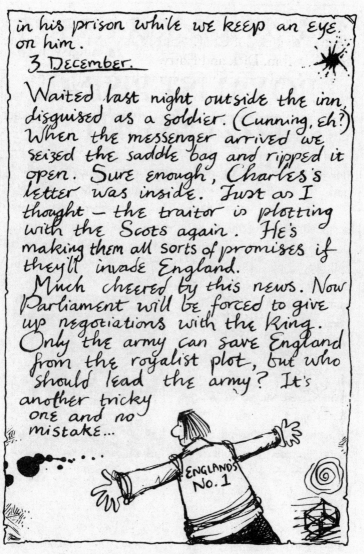

ENGLAND'S NO.1

As Oliver expected, Parliament turned to him once more to save the day. And once again he showed that on the battlefield he was invincible.

THE CAVALIER CRYER

26 AUGUST 1648

ROYALIST RISING FIZZLES OUT

In only six months Charles's hopes of becoming the comeback king have been shattered. News of the Scots' defeat by Cromwell was swiftly followed by Colchester's surrender in the south. In the end the Second Civil War has been little more than a feeble whimper.

The king hoped for better this summer when royalist risings were staged in Wales, Essex and Kent. Half the navy also cheered for the king as the Scots prepared to invade. But once more royalist hopes have been crushed on the rock of Cromwell. His men were outnumbered two to one, but the Scots' commander, the Duke of Hamilton, was no match for the man they call 'Ironsides'. Hamilton botched the battle by failing to keep his army together. As they approached Preston the cavalry and infantry were miles apart and failed to find each other in the dark.

Scots in the dark

Cromwell pursued them north of Warrington and beat them. 'What were we fighting for anyway?' complained one muddy Scots soldier after the battle.

Dog meat

Meanwhile, Colchester had been under siege for two months by General Fairfax. The civilians inside were reduced to eating cats and dogs to keep them alive.

No place for a dog

When news came of Cromwell's victory the royalists realized their position was hopeless and surrendered. They got no mercy from Roundhead General Fairfax. Two of the leaders of the revolt were shot and a third, Lord Capel, has been sent to the Tower of London to await execution.

It's all grim news for King Charles. If he's going to survive the peace negotiations, he'll need to keep his head.

The bum Parliament

Charles didn't play much part in the Second Civil War. He was still in prison on the Isle of Wight, remember. He did try another of his famous escape routines, but he was too big to squeeze through the narrow window. (Maybe it was all that stodgy prison food.)

Meanwhile Parliament, fearing a military takeover, urged the king to agree peace terms. This was probably Charles's last chance, but as usual he played for time. In his own daft mind he was playing a complex game of chess. But no one else understood the rules.

As for Oliver, he'd lost patience with the dithering king and with Parliament. On 6 December Colonel Thomas Pride – a former beer-cart driver – marched into the House of Commons with a troop of soldiers. He prevented 200 MPs from taking their seats. Anyone who protested was locked in a tavern for the night. The 150 members who remained just happened to be mostly Independents (like Cromwell). People rudely called them the Rump Parliament, since it was a bum deal all round.

Once again, Oliver denied the outrage was carried out on his orders. Was it just a coincidence that he turned up in London only hours afterwards?

The army were now in control and Oliver said the time had come to act. This was bad news for Charles, but good news for axe-makers.

I tell you we shall cut off the king's head with the crown on it.

Charles was taken to Windsor Castle. He appealed to his subjects that he was blameless and had only wanted peace all along. The rumour spread that he was doomed. Even many of the king's enemies felt this was going too far. Many in London felt the country was going to the dogs, as the words of a street ballad show.

There is no such thing as a Bishop or King,
Or Peer, but in name or show.
Come clowns and come boys, come hobbledehoys,
Come females and each degree,
Stretch out your throats, bringing in your votes,
And make good the anarchy...
Then let's have King Charles, says George.
Nay, we'll have his son, says Hugh.
Nay, let's have none, says jabbering Joan.
Nay, we'll all be kings, says Prue.

Heads you lose

Of course, before the king could be bumped off he had to be given a 'fair' trial. Funnily enough, no one was eager to volunteer for the court. (Sentencing kings to death is a risky business.) Men like Sir Thomas Fairfax suddenly found they had to be out of London that week.

Two top judges turned down the chance to be President of the Court. The judge who accepted the job – John Bradshaw – took no chances. Take a look at his hat.

REINFORCED STEEL IN CASE ANYONE TAKES A POT-SHOT

Of the 150 'judges' first appointed to the court, half of them made excuses. Cromwell's name was at the top of the list and he had no such qualms. Perhaps he even recorded the trial in the pages of his diary?

Oliver's Secret Diary

20 January 1649

Trial began today. The court is so packed that spectators climb the walls to sit on the windowsills for a better view. Well! No one can say we're doing this great work in secret.

The prisoner wore a black velvet cloak, with the star of the Garter gleaming on his sleeve. His cheeks were sunken, his hair grey, his eyes

Shadowed. To tell the truth, he looked pathetically old. At one point, when the charge was read, the silver knob on the king's cane fell off. He just stood there, obviously waiting for his page or someone else to pick it up. Nobody did. Eventually he was forced to stoop and pick it up himself. It's probably the first time he's bent down for anything.

27 January

The King refuses to plead guilty! In fact, he won't plead anything at all since he says our court has no authority. When Judge Bradshaw said his accusers were 'the people of England' a voice from the gallery shouted, 'Not a quarter of them! Cromwell is a traitor!' The soldiers were about to fire their muskets at this rogue when they realized it was Lady Fairfax, wife of my general and commanding officer. Embarrassing!

STEADY ON, DEAR...

28 January

I swear the King has the hardest heart of any man on Earth. Today he even demanded to give a speech before we sentenced him to death.

The sentence was finally read out. 'This court does judge that the said Charles Stuart, as a tyrant, traitor, murderer and a public enemy shall be put to death by the severing of his head from his body.' Seemed fair enough to me.

But even then the King insisted on interrupting!

'I may speak after the sentence by your favour, Sir! Hold!' the fool gabbled, till he had to be led away by my gallant soldiers. 'Execution! Justice! Execution!' they cried out (which took no end of practice last night).

'Poor creatures,' Charles mocked, 'for sixpence they will say as much of their own commanders.'

You'd think a man in his position would hold his tongue before it gets him into more trouble.

The throne room

Poor Charles was treated rudely through the whole trial. Once he was spat on by spectators as he left the court. Even more humiliating, a guard was ordered to stay with him at all times. Charles couldn't even go to the loo on his own!

As for Cromwell, he'd decided Charles had to go and he didn't appear to lose any sleep over the matter. There were 59 signatures on the death warrant and Cromwell's name was third on the list. When the time came, one judge, Sir Richard Ingoldsby, refused to sign. Cromwell ran at him across the room, dragged him to the table and laughed while he held his hand down to trace his signature. And if you think that was unfeeling, what about this? When Cromwell had signed his own name he started an ink-fight with his pal, Henry Marten. Soon the two of them were smearing ink on each other's faces like naughty schoolboys. You'd have thought they were scribbling notes in class rather than signing the king's death warrant!

For a Puritan, Oliver had a very odd sense of humour. But for Charles it was no laughing matter. His time was up.

THE CAVALIER CRYER

30 JANUARY 1649

IT'S THE CHOP FOR CHARLIE!

'Behold the head of a traitor!' cried the executioner just before two o' clock this afternoon. No cheer came from the watching crowd. As one witness said, 'There was such a groan by the thousands there present as I never heard before and desire I may never hear again.' King Charles, England's rightful monarch, had just been executed.

Shirty

The king may have had his critics in his lifetime, but even his enemies admit that he died like a prince. The weather was so icy Charles secretly wore two shirts, worried that people might see him trembling and imagine he was afraid. At half past one he climbed on to the scaffold where iron chains and ropes were prepared in case he struggled. But it wasn't Charles who was scared. His two executioners wore masks and false beards and wigs in case they were identified. Cromwell and his crew of traitors were said to be 'at a prayer meeting'.

Choppers in disguise

Last words

Charles read his last dignified words from a piece of paper: 'All the world knows that I never did begin a war first with the two Houses of Parliament,' he said. 'I tell you that I am the martyr of the people.' He took off his doublet, prayed for a moment and rested his neck on the block. The blow fell quickly. Soon after, the crowd surged forward. Many of them carried off handfuls of hair and blood as trophies. Even the bloodstained chopping block was cut into chips and sold for souvenirs.

So perished King Charles who 'died greater than he lived'. With His Highness gone what kind of mercy can England expect now from the likes of heartless Cromwell?

King Charles (1600–49)

Mystery visit

Charles was buried at Windsor Castle, in the same vault as Henry VIII. It's hard to think of two English kings who were more different. Big Henry was a bullying tyrant, shy Charles was a hopeless ditherer. Henry's hobby was collecting the heads of his wives while Charles ended up headless himself. England had changed a lot in a hundred years!

There is a story that while the king's body lay in its coffin at Whitehall, Oliver Cromwell paid a visit. At least it may have been Cromwell. At two o' clock in the morning, a mysterious stranger opened the door, his face muffled in his cloak. He approached the coffin, gazed at the king's body and shook his head. The stranger uttered only two words: 'Cruel necessity.' Then he vanished into the night. Was it Cromwell? It's the kind of thing that he might have done. Perhaps secretly he regretted what happened to Charles, but if so, he kept it to himself.

WARTS AND ALL ~ AWFUL OMENS

Charles probably had plenty of regrets as he stood on the scaffold that cold January morning. Maybe he thought back to some of the omens he'd ignored. There were quite a few...

It's all in the stars

William Lily started out as a common servant but ended up as the most famous astrologer in seventeenth century England. An astrologer is someone who tells the future by looking at the stars and wizard Lily certainly had a sparkling track record.

For starters, at the beginning of the Civil War, Lily studied the king's star-chart and warned that 1645 would be a bad year for Charles. On the very day

Lily's prediction appeared in *The Starry Messenger* – 14 June 1645 – Charles lost the battle of Naseby and effectively the whole war.

Still, better luck next time. Two years later when Charles escaped from the army, he consulted Lily for the best place to hide. Lily told him that Essex was his best bolt-hole and got paid £20 for his services. Charles, however, ignored the advice and fled to the Isle of Wight – where he landed himself back in jail.

Never mind, third time lucky, perhaps? When Charles was at his lowest, Lily advised him to sign peace terms with the army and hope the public would grow tired of his enemies. Did Charles listen this time? Not on your life! Soon after, Charles was history.

Don't go bust

While at Whitehall Charles had a bust made of himself by the famous sculptor, Bernini. Just at the moment the bust was unveiled, a hawk flew by carrying a dead bird in its beak. A drop of blood fell from the bird and landed on the throat of Charles's marble head. Not long after, Charles and his real head parted company.

Beware the shaven heads

In any top ten of soothsayers and stargazers, Nostradamus's name would come near the top. The prophet made predictions about everything from Napoleon's fate to the date of the Great Fire of London.

One of his famous predictions sounds like a riddle:

> *The unworthy man will be chased from the English kingdom.*
> *The counsellor through anger will be burnt.*
> *His followers will stoop to such depths,*
> *That the Pretender will almost be received.*

If Charles was the unworthy man who lost his kingdom, then Archbishop Laud was his trusted counsellor (though actually, he was beheaded not burnt). The followers who stooped so low were the Scots who sold the king back to Parliament, and the Pretender would be Cromwell who was almost accepted as king.

Nostradamus even predicted the way Charles would die: *'The parliament of London will put their king to death... He will die because of the shaven heads in council.'*

Salt of the earth

Even after his death, Charles had rotten luck. Did you know, for instance, that 150 years later he came back as a salt-cellar?

Charles, remember, was buried in a vault at Windsor Castle along with Henry VIII. For a long time both coffins were lost, until in 1813 the vault was accidentally discovered by workers who made a hole in the wall. The coffin was opened and the body examined by the royal surgeon, Sir Henry Halford. Halford, like Cromwell, had rather an odd taste in practical jokes. He secretly stole the king's fourth cervical vertebra (part of the neckbone) which had been sliced through by the axe. For the next thirty years he loved to shock his friends at dinner parties by using the king's vertebra as a salt-cellar.

So much for Charles and his mouldy old bones. For now, Oliver Cromwell was left as the most powerful man in England. Yet history often comes full circle. Only a dozen years later it would be Cromwell's turn to rest his neck on the block. Even though the chop would come a little too late.

TIMELINE: OLIVER RULES

1649: THE MONARCHY IS ABOLISHED BY ACT OF PARLIAMENT. START OF COMMONWEALTH.

THEY'RE CERTAINLY COMMON...

1651: SCOTS CROWN CHARLIE'S BOY AS KING. BATTLE OF WORCESTER— SCOTS 0, CROMWELL 2. CHARLES II MAKES DARING ESCAPE TO FRANCE.

HEE HEE! CAN'T CATCH ME!

1652: TAKE A BREAK— FIRST ENGLISH COFFEE HOUSE OPENS. PRAYER BOOK REPLACED BY PURITAN DIRECTORY.

PHONE A PURITAN

1653: CROMWELL GIVES PARLIAMENT A KICK UP THE RUMP — AND BECOMES LORD PROTECTOR.

MPs — WHO NEEDS 'EM?

1654: WAR WITH SPAIN— ENGLAND CAPTURES JAMAICA.

AND WE'VE ALSO CAPTURED THIS JAM MAKER

1656: FIRST ENGLISH OPERA HITS THE HIGH NOTES

SHE SHOULD BE BANNED!

1657: THREE CHEERS! FIRST CHOCOLATE SHOP OPENS IN LONDON. OLIVER OFFERED THE CROWN BUT TURNS IT DOWN.

I'D RATHER HAVE A MARS BAR

1658: DEATH OF CROMWELL. CROMWELL JUNIOR TAKES OVER.

THANKS DAD...

1660: RICHARD CROMWELL RESIGNS — COMMONWEALTH COLLAPSES.

DOWN WITH DICK

Boo!

WHOOPS!

Bring back the KING!

1661: OLIVER DUG UP. HIS HEAD GOES ON ITS TRAVELS.

I FANCY GREECE THIS YEAR...

OLIVER AND THE KILLJOY COMMONWEALTH

> *No man rises so high as he who knows not whither he goes.*

Cromwell always denied harbouring any ambitions to become the most powerful man in Britain. Of course, he *would* say that. His enemies thought differently. Many who fought with him in the war afterwards claimed his head was swollen by power.

Yet if Cromwell had a master plan to become King Oliver I, he was pretty good at hiding it. In the beginning Oliver hoped England could be ruled by Parliament, but he soon discovered why Charles had tried ruling by himself.

The clueless Commonwealth

Soon after Charles I died, the monarchy and the House of Lords were abolished by an Act of Parliament. In their place, England was declared a Commonwealth.

What exactly was a Commonwealth? No one was too sure since England had never had one before. The only certain thing, was that England was the only country in Europe with an empty throne.

Oliver towered above everyone else in the land. But all kinds of problems faced him on every side.

The most dangerous threat to the new Commonwealth was the Irish revolt. As usual Cromwell didn't waste time on words, he took action – and pretty ugly action at that.

By now all royalist rags had been torn up and replaced by Commonwealth newspapers. So here's how a pro-Cromwell newspaper might have reported his Irish campaign.

THE RIGHTEOUS ROUNDHEAD

12 OCTOBER 1649

IRISH REBELLION CRUSHED

Oliver Cromwell has put down the Irish rebellion in scenes more brutal than anything seen in the Civil War. In two months, the greatest general alive has laid siege to the towns of Drogheda and Wexford and crushed the enemy.

Cromwell came to Ireland, sworn to revenge a massacre of English Protestants eight years ago. He is also well known for his hatred of Irish Catholicism. But no one expected such a ferocious start to his campaign.

Hell to pay

Sir Arthur Aston, in charge of Drogheda, boasted, 'if you can take Drogheda, you can take hell'. He'd obviously not met Cromwell before. Poor Aston was left without a leg to stand on. In the battle one of Cromwell's

116

men pinched Aston's wooden leg and used it to bash his brains out. His men didn't fare any better. Around 2,600 people were killed – including every priest in the town and some civilians.

Wexford was dealt with in the same brutal fashion. General Cromwell stands by his methods. 'I am persuaded that this is a righteous judgment of God upon these barbarous wretches who have stained their hands in so much innocent blood,' he said, before heading off to wash his hands.

Cromwell's cruelty would make him a hate-figure in Ireland for all time. Back in England, however, he returned a conquering hero. Cromwell was now Commander-in-Chief of the Army.

But there was little time for congratulations. Soon the Scots were on the march and threatening to restore Charles II to the English throne. Yes, it was time for yet another battle – if Oliver could just find the enemy.

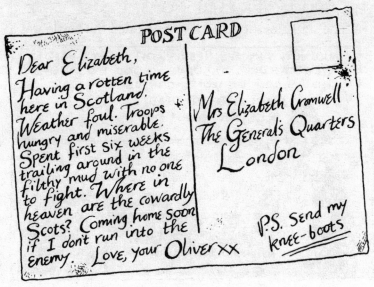

POST CARD

Dear Elizabeth,
Having a rotten time here in Scotland. Weather foul. Troops hungry and miserable. Spent first six weeks trailing around in the filthy mud with no one to fight. Where in heaven are the cowardly Scots? Coming home soon if I don't run into the enemy. Love, your Oliver xx

Mrs Elizabeth Cromwell
The General's Quarters
London

P.S. Send my knee-boots

In fact Cromwell's Scottish campaign came close to disaster. By the time he turned for home, his army was exhausted and starving. Things couldn't get any worse could they? Of course they could! At Dunbar the Scots army finally showed up with 22,000 men. Oliver in comparison had only 11,000 and most of them were only fit to crawl into bed. He was trapped. For the first time it looked like a thrashing for the invincible Ironsides. He wrote home: 'we have much hope in the Lord'. Which was just as well since he needed a miracle.

Being Cromwell he got one. (No wonder he thought God was on his side!) The Scottish Parliament meddled in the battle plans, ordering their commander to abandon his (very strong) position on a hill and take up a (very weak) position on level ground. Oliver, watching, must have practically jumped for joy. At four in the morning he launched a surprise attack and routed the enemy before breakfast.

The statistics show just how one-sided the battle was.

AND HERE ARE THE RESULTS OF TODAY'S BATTLE: **SCOTLAND**: 3,000 DEAD, 10,000 PRISONERS AND 15,000 WEAPONS CAPTURED. **ENGLAND**: 20 DEAD. **RESULT**: AWAY WIN.

Cromwell – as ever – claimed it was all God's doing.

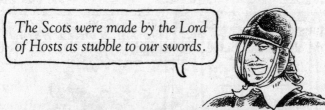

> *The Scots were made by the Lord of Hosts as stubble to our swords.*

His only regret was that Charles II didn't show up for the battle. The following January Charles Junior was crowned King of Scotland at Scone. (All Scottish kings were crowned at Scone, having tea and cakes afterwards.) In August young Charlie marched south with an army, hoping to reach London. But Cromwell caught up with him at Worcester. It was like a re-run of all those old Civil War battles and once again Ironsides proved he was unbeatable.

Charles II was no military genius, but at least he'd inherited one of his father's talents…

His flight after the battle of Worcester is a ripping adventure story.

Here's slippery Charlie himself to tell it.

119

THE GREAT ESCAPE

Charles II finally quit England on 14 October 1651. By that time many people were fed up with the Commonwealth, and wondering if kings weren't such a bad idea after all. The Rump Parliament was still in power and it was dominated by prim Puritans. Since the beginning of the Civil War they'd launched a crusade to rid society of a shocking evil.

A traditional rhyme describes Puritans pretty accurately:

We are a serious people, grim and full of cares,
And melancholy as cats, as glum as hares.

Puritans believed that the purpose of life was to serve God and to work hard. Anything that sounded like fun they thought was a sinful temptation. As you can imagine, this made everyday life pretty dreary.

Lousy laws

In the ten years between 1640 and 1650 a whole range of killjoy laws were dreamed up by Parliament. Here are some of them.

One thing that's missing from the list, you'll notice, is a law against drinking. Although Puritans enforced strict licensing laws they couldn't actually stop people drinking altogether. For instance, if you walked along London's Fleet Street in 1650 you could call in at 74 taverns and alehouses along the way.

Alehouses were also a popular place to enjoy a quiet smoke and this was regarded as a positively healthy past-time! Cromwell himself was a pipe smoker, like many Puritans. One doctor declared: 'If moderately and seasonably taken ... (tobacco) is good for many things, it helps digestion taken a while after meat; a leaf or two steeped overnight in a little white wine is a vomit that never fails in its operations'.

Work, rest and no play

Imagine how dull life would be if you lived during Cromwell's Commonwealth. Six days a week you'd go to work or school. Sundays were a day of rest – which meant just that. You couldn't cook, clean, play or do just about anything except go to church. Cromwell's soldiers made sure that everyone kept the Sabbath (Sunday). You could get in trouble just for breathing. One man was fined ten shillings for walking to the next village to hear a sermon, while a woman was put in the stocks just for mending her dress.

Of course children who broke the Sabbath weren't put in the stocks...

Generously the government declared the second Tuesday of every month a holiday 'for reasonable recreation'. But what on earth did they mean? The Puritans had banned almost every kind of entertainment.

Here's how the lousy laws affected everyday life.

Wicked maypoles

Maypoles were banned on the grounds that they encouraged music, dancing and other shocking practices. But not everyone obeyed and in 1658 it was reported that the citizens of Bury St Edmunds 'ran horribly mad upon a maypole'.

Moany Christmas

Puritans regarded all festivals as 'born of the devil'. Christmas was especially scorned as a 'heathen' festival and just another excuse for people to have FUN. Why couldn't the English observe Christmas 'without drinking, roaring, healthing, dicing, carding, masques and stageplays?' grumbled one Puritan.

Christmas under the Puritans was turned into a fast day by law. That meant going without food and thinking about your sins. Eating Christmas dinner was strictly forbidden. One year soldiers actually went from house to house checking that no one was secretly cooking a fat goose or tucking into naughty mince pies.

Most people resented the loss of their Christmas merry-making. By law, churches were supposed to close on Christmas Day while shops were meant to stay open as usual. Yet in 1647 many London shops closed their doors and the Lord Mayor was jeered so loudly his horse bolted with fright. In Canterbury people played football in the streets and ten thousand men passed a resolution that 'if they could not have their Christmas Day they would have the King back on his throne'.

Blasted swearing

Swearing was outlawed by an Act of Parliament in 1650 which set down fines for people who were caught cursing. In the interests of fairness rich people got fined more than the poor. A duke who swore was fined a whacking 30 shillings while a commoner had to cough up just 3 shillings and 4d. That may not sound much but in 1650 a shilling was a day's wages for a labourer. If you couldn't pay your fine you were put in the stocks and left for the day.

Given the tough punishments, you'd think people were using some shocking swear words. Of course we can't print them all but here are a couple that we're allowed to show you...

(Note: Please don't show this page to your parents in case they complain to the publishers.)

Mild music

So what *did* Puritans do to enjoy themselves? Well, if you don't count listening to sermons, they were quietly fond of music. Of course you couldn't go totally wild and sing on the Lord's day or tap your feet to the church organ (mainly because all organs had been removed). Nevertheless you could enjoy music at home. Cromwell himself was a great music-lover and raised a few eyebrows with the music and dancing at his daughter's wedding in 1657. In fact he liked music so much that he had the organ from Magdalen College at Oxford University brought to Hampton Court so he could hear it played more often.

The Commonwealth was also responsible for the showing of the first English opera. It was called *The Siege of Rhodes* and was so popular that a second opera followed soon after. This one was called *The Cruelty of the Spaniards in Peru*.

Old Noll

As far as Oliver is concerned, this is all leaping ahead a bit. When we left him, it was 1651 and he'd just nobbled Charles II's chances of getting his crown back. Old Noll – as he was nicknamed – had been a soldier for ten years. In that time he'd risen from being a common captain to the top brass of Parliament's army.

Now it was time to turn his back on war and sort out the peace. But it was one thing to win a battle, running a country was a tougher problem.

To begin with there was still the thorny problem of religion. The Anglican church had been chucked out during the war, but what should replace it? Lots of groups had their own ideas. In fact, in the 1650s England was awash with every kind of religious nutcase you could imagine. Take a look at a couple of the barmy religions on offer.

WARTS AND ALL - RAVING RELIGIONS

Ranters

Most religions agree that loving your neighbour is a good thing. Equally they say, stealing your neighbour's chickens or his wife are not good things. The Ranters were different. In a nutshell they said that sin (doing bad things) can't be bad.

Their argument went like this:

GOD MADE EVERYTHING, SO GOD MADE SIN, THEREFORE SIN MUST BE GOOD, RIGHT?

ER... WRONG, BUT I'M NOT SURE WHERE..

These raving ideas led to all kinds of things. One of the Ranter leaders, Laurence Clarkson, declared:

There is no such thing as drunkeness, adultery and theft in God.

The Ranters claimed that you were free to do anything you liked and God bless your thieving heart. Naturally this new brand of religion was very popular, especially with the poor who were only too happy to pinch a few of their neighbours' chickens. Parliament was so worried by the barmy Ranters that it passed a Blasphemy Law in 1650 to try and stamp them out.

Diggers
The Diggers were all about, um ... digging. They wanted to restore the fruits of the earth (not to mention the vegetables) to God's people. To fulfil their plan, they dug up any land they could lay their hands on and planted seeds and beans. As one writer described it:

> *They invited all to come in and help them and promised them meat and drink, and clothes; they threatened to pull down park pales (fences) and to lay all open, and threatened the neighbours that they will shortly make them all come up the hill and work.*

Not surprisingly landowners didn't like anyone digging their land up, whether they were 'God's people' or not.

On 19 April 1649 the Diggers' big dig-in was broken up by Cromwell's troops and all their tender seedlings torn up. It was a pity but perhaps they were before their time. If they'd been alive today they might have had their own gardening series on TV.

AND NEXT WEEK WE'LL BE DIGGING UP NEXT DOOR'S PATIO...

A kick up the Rump

Raving religions were a nuisance, but they were only one of Cromwell's problems. The real trouble was that Parliament wasn't any better at running the country than Charles I had been.

Originally the army had got sick of the Long Parliament (13 years is too long for anyone) and replaced it with the Rump. Now Cromwell got fed up with waiting for the new Parliament to pass useful reforms. They didn't hold elections or bring down taxes, in fact most people agreed that they were a pain in the rump.

In April 1653 Cromwell marched into the House of Commons. He was in such a temper he hadn't even bothered to change out of his old grey socks.

Oliver's Secret Diary

10 April 1653

Arrived at Commons in a foul mood. Tried to speak calmly but soon lost my temper. Found I was striding up and down, stamping the floor and shouting.

'Call yourself a Parliament? I say you are no Parliament! In the name of God, go!'

One of the MPs actually tried to calm me down. The nerve of it! That was the last straw! I called in the soldiers. Six musketeers from my regiment marched in and dragged the speaker out of his chair. In half an hour I'd

> cleared the whole house of the rogues. Most of them took one look at me and made for the door pretty quickly. Lucky for them!

Does this scene feel somehow familiar? The House of Commons invaded by a troop of soldiers. Ah yes, that was the trick Charles I tried in 1642, sparking off a civil war. This time it was different of course, or that's what Cromwell said. It was ironic really. He'd fought a war to stop the king behaving like a dictator and he'd ended up behaving like one himself. For all his high ambitions, Cromwell's power rested on the barrel of a gun. These days we'd call it a military coup.

Barmy Parliaments

The country was now without a Rump, but it needed *something* to sit in Parliament. Enter the Barebones Parliament. At this point let's pause for a moment. All these Parliaments can get a bit confusing and why do they have such barmy names? A handy guide to Potty Puritan Parliaments will help you sort them out.

WARTS AND ALL ~ POTTY PARLIAMENTS

NAME OF PARLIAMENT	WHY?	CLAIM TO FAME
1640 SHORT	LASTED LESS THAN A MONTH	SHORTEST ON RECORD
1640-1653 LONG	LASTED 13 LONG YEARS	ONLY PARLIAMENT TO SIT THROUGH A CIVIL WAR
1648-53 RUMP	REAR END OF THE LONG PARLIAMENT	RUDEST ON RECORD
1653 BAREBONES	AFTER MP CALLED BAREBONES	FIRST SAINTS TO SIT IN PARLIAMENT
1653-58 Cromwell rules as Lord Protector		IF YOU WANT A JOB DOING...

The name game

Of all the potty Parliaments to sit in the House of Commons, the Barebones was the biggest flop. Cromwell's idea must have seemed brilliant at the time. He would hand-pick a Parliament of honest, godly men (just like himself). In fact they were so good they were to be known as a Parliament of Saints (not a word you often hear used about MPs). No doubt they were very godly and honest, but none of them had a clue about running a country. In less than a year the Barebones Parliament collapsed.

Its nickname came from one of its unimportant members who went under the glorious name of Obadiah Praise-be-to-God Barebones. No honestly, that was his real name! Puritans in the seventeenth century were fond of pious sounding names. Sometimes they plucked them at random from the Bible, or worse they made up names for their poor miserable children. Imagine being landed with some of these first names:

A nose by any other name

Oliver was given lots of funny nicknames by his enemies. Most of them referred to his colossal conk which by middle age was like a glowing beacon in the middle of his face.

Even Oliver's supporters were obsessed with the size of his conk. One declared:

If he's not honest I'll never trust a man with a big nose again.

But big nose or not, Oliver was now the only man capable of ruling Britain. (And the only one with an army behind him.) With a series of Parliaments ending in a shambles and Charles II waiting in France, it was now up to Old Noll to hold the reins of power alone. It was only a short hop, skip and jump to becoming king. The question was, would he become...?

OLIVER THE FIRST?

THE RIGHTEOUS ROUNDHEAD

16 DECEMBER 1653

OLIVER PROTECTOR

Cromwell – Protection racket

Oliver Cromwell was today proclaimed Lord Protector of England, Scotland and Ireland.

It's the latest episode in a meteoric rags-to-riches rise for Cromwell who started off a country farmer. (His enemies claim he was a common brewer but this is ale nonsense.)

As Lord Protector, Cromwell will have wide ranging powers – backed by a Council of State.

Rumours

Since the Barebones Parliament voted to dismiss itself four days ago, rumours have spread that Cromwell has set his cap at becoming king. Friends say the idea has been raised but Cromwell is not keen to jump into the shoes of Charles I. Look what happened to him!

Still, from now on Cromwell will be addressed as His Highness the Lord Protector and he'll move into the king's old palace at Whitehall. He may not wear a crown, but some say he means to live like a king.

The warty Roundhead

Let's take a look at Oliver at the height of his power. (It's mainly downhill from now on.) It was the custom of the age for portraits to be painted in heroic style. Armoured knights on dashing chargers were the usual sort of thing. Typically Oliver had to be different. He didn't want to be painted as a romantic hero. If he had to have his portrait done he wanted a plain, honest picture. The tale goes that he threatened not to pay the artist a penny unless the portrait showed him 'warts and all' (which is where the saying comes from).

Oliver the wrinkly

Cromwell was nearly 55 years old. In the Stuart age that would have qualified him for his pensioner's bus pass. There was no older leader in the whole of Europe. Then again, Oliver had always been a late starter.

How did his subjects feel about having the ex-general to rule them? They were certainly tired of the mess Parliament was making, but many believed Cromwell was getting too big for his boots. At the ceremony to install the Lord Protector there was polite applause but it wasn't exactly wild cheering. Soldiers lined the streets on the way to Whitehall to make sure no one attacked the new Protector.

Many thought Cromwell was just biding his time until he could become King Oliver I. Royalists weren't willing to stand by and see that happen. They believed that if they could only bump off Cromwell then the Commonwealth would crumble and Charles II would make a comeback.

Killing Cromwell

Killing Cromwell wasn't an easy matter. The Lord Protector was well protected. He had his own secret service to foil dirty plots. (More about that later.) It was said that Cromwell often changed his travel plans, never slept in the same bed twice, and was guarded day and night by soldiers armed with swords and pistols.

IT'S TO PROTECT ME FROM MY MANY FANS...

None of this stopped Oliver's enemies trying their luck. There were several dastardly plots, but all were doomed to failure.

A flying brick

The first attempt to kill Cromwell was a pretty clumsy one. It happened when he attended a banquet thrown in his honour by the City of London. The streets were decorated with flags and streamers, the church bells were ringing, even Oliver himself had his usual brown suit embroidered with gold. But the festivities were nearly spoiled by a Miss Greenville who chucked a brick at the Protector's coach. Fortunately for Oliver he wasn't poking his nose out at the time, otherwise she couldn't have missed.

A clever ambush

A more serious plot followed in 1654. A former royalist colonel, John Gerard, planned to seize the Protector with a company of 30 men, as Cromwell travelled between Whitehall and Hampton Court. Luckily for Oliver, his master spy found out the plot. Instead of going by coach Cromwell took a barge down the Thames. It left his ambushers looking pretty silly with no one to ambush. Gerard's plot got him the chop, though his behaviour was 'sprightly and Cavalier-like' till the end, according to the newspapers.

A cunning plan – or three

Another plot came to light three years later. In fact it wasn't one but three murky plots – just to make sure.

The first plot involved two men called Cecil and Sindercombe blowing Cromwell to bits as his coach went by. They were going to use lethal 'screwed guns' containing twelve bullets and a slug (not the squashy variety). This plot was foiled by Cromwell again switching routes at the last minute.

The second plot was to nobble old Copper Nose in Hyde Park. The old soldier Cecil made cunning plans for a quick escape after the murder. He had the hinges of a gate filed through, wore special lightweight clothes and even borrowed a swift horse. Unfortunately the horse caught a cold and the plan was put to bed with a hot water bottle.

The final plot took no chances, it was time for the big boom. The plan was to blow up Cromwell's palace at Whitehall, by planting explosives in the chapel. At this point one of the plotters' accomplices in the palace guard gave the game away. A basket of suspicious-looking matches and 'active flaming stuff' was discovered in the chapel. The bungling Cecil soon confessed. Sindercombe was arrested but escaped the chop. He preferred to take poison right under the nose of his jailers.

Cromwell's narrow escape was celebrated by a service of thanksgiving at London's Banqueting House. After the service an old staircase collapsed under the weight of the guests, injuring several people, including Cromwell's son!

Sneaky spies and lemon letters

James Bond would have been at home in Cromwell's day. Sneaky spies were common in the seventeenth century and Oliver had the best secret service in Europe. The Protectorate was rumoured to spend £70,000 a year on its spy service. Since the average spy's pay was only £10 a month, Cromwell must have employed an army of them.

The sneakiest of all was Cromwell's master spy – John Thurloe. Thurloe was an artful lawyer who rose to be one of the most powerful men in England. As Postmaster General it was easy for him to read everybody's letters. He used a wide network of spies and informers to gather information on Cromwell's enemies. Sometimes his spies sent secret messages written in lemon juice (the invisible ink of the day!). Cardinal Mazarin (the French chief minister) admitted that he never understood how Thurloe knew so many of his secrets.

While Thurloe's spies were sending secret messages from the French court, the French had their own spies at Cromwell's court. It wasn't safe to trust your own mother – especially if you caught her squeezing a lemon.

At the height of his powers Thurloe wore so many hats he needed six heads.

Here's a rare picture of him.

The major generals

It wasn't only secret plots that threatened the Protector. In 1655 there was another rising against the government led by a royalist colonel called Penruddock.

143

Cromwell's response was to turn to the army again. He appointed 11 'major generals' to keep order. Each of them was given a different part of the country to police and their powers ranged from enforcing the Sabbath to closing theatres. Imagine what the job ad might have looked like:

WANTED: MAJOR GENERALS

Reliable chaps who know a rebellion when they see one and can put a stop to it on the double. You should be a dab hand at disarming rebels and ferreting out thieves, robbers, highwaymen and riff-raff in general.

You should have strong views on the wickedness of horse-racing, cock-fighting, gaming houses, bear-baiting, stage plays and all that kind of tommy-rot. Good sense of humour essential.

Send an application together with the size of your moustache to: OLIVER CROMWELL-LORD PROTECTOR, Whitehall, London.

With the country already a fun-free zone, you can guess how popular the major generals were. Their powers were so wide that they could imprison people merely for being drunk or starting an argument. One old royalist soldier was brought for trial on the grounds that he had 'gone awooing to two maids' and borrowed money from them on the promise of marriage. (Admittedly he did have a wife in London that he forgot to mention.)

Some major generals were stricter than others. Charles Worsley in Lancashire banned all horse racing, while Edward Whalley in Lincolnshire was very fond of racing himself. Whalley boasted:

> *I may truly say you can ride over all Nottinghamshire and not see a beggar or a wandering rogue.*

So where were all the beggars? Rotting in prison for the 'wicked' offence of being poor and hungry!

Living like a king

Cromwell ruled the land with an iron fist, but did that mean he lived a dull, simple life himself? Far from it. At Cromwell's court in Whitehall Palace he lived like a king. Not only had he moved into King Charles's old house, he'd also employed his old servants on the same wages. They included grooms, chaplains, doctors, cooks, barge masters and dozens of footmen.

When the Swedish ambassador visited he got the red-carpet treatment. Cromwell had his guest entertained with music and taken stag hunting. He rounded it all off by playing a round of croquet with the ambassador himself. Not bad for a killjoy Puritan.

And Oliver knew how to throw a party too. There was nothing miserly or dull about the wedding party for his daughter Frances in 1657. In fact, by all accounts, Oliver got a little carried away…

Oliver's Secret Diary.

11 November 1657

A day of mirth and frolic! Haven't enjoyed myself so much since daubing myself with dung when I was a lad!

The wedding party got underway at five with the modest entertainment I'd ordered for the occasion — a simple band of 48 violins and 50 trumpets. We were soon all on the floor dancing — men and women together (which I dare say will cause a scandal in some places). I even saw my wife kicking up her heels with the Earl of Newport.

No wedding is complete without a few jests and who better than the bride's father to provide them? How the ladies shrieked when I started throwing sherry over their fine dresses!

Sometimes I put a sticky sweetmeat on a chair just as a guest was about to sit down. How I howled when they stood up with it stuck to their bottom!

My son-in-law, Robert Rich, begged me not to go any further, but I replied by plucking off his wig. I pretended to throw it in the fire and ended up sitting on it. That brought the house down, I can tell you!

Got to bed about 5 a.m. Party moves on to Warwick tomorrow. Lucky for everyone I'll be there to liven things up!

EEEEEk!

OH JOY!

This may not sound like the behaviour of a Lord Protector (the pranks are all true) but Cromwell was no ordinary ruler. He could be solemn one minute and having a pillow fight with his pals the next. What's more, he'd come a long way since his first speech in Parliament wearing a baggy old suit. For his daughter's wedding Oliver cut a dash in grey velvet breeches and doublet, a pair of silk stockings, Spanish leather shoes and gold laced garters. Visitors to his court remarked that plain old Noll had even started to dress like a king.

Arty Oliver

Music wasn't the only entertainment that flourished at Cromwell's court. The London theatres may have closed but Cromwell liked to encourage talented artists, poets and writers. Here's a guide to some of the stars who sparkled at Oliver's court.

Andrew Marvell

Occupation: Poet.

A blooming marvel? Son of a schoolteacher, so he had a tough start in life. Nevertheless Marvell could turn a neat verse and made his name with racy love poems.

Best career move: Wrote a toadying ode about Cromwell on his return from Ireland. (Sample: *And if we would speak true, Much to the man is due.*)

Worst career move: The ode also contained an admiring verse about the dignified death of Charles I. Marvell's poem must have raised a few eyebrows, but Cromwell didn't punish him. Maybe he never read the poem anyway.

John Milton

Occupation: Another poet. (Poetry was one of the few arts prim Puritans approved of.)

More toady odes then? The epic poem was more Milton's line. See his great work *Paradise Lost* – or don't if you prefer poems that you can read in a day.

Best career move: Got a day job under Oliver's Protectorate as 'Secretary to Foreign Tongues' on a

salary of £288 a year with a flat at Whitehall thrown in.
Odd fact: Although Milton was a prim Puritan he liked music so much that he had an organ installed in his own home. Perhaps he amused his chums in the evenings playing Puritan chart toppers.

James Harrington
Occupation: Philosopher and writer.
What was he all about then?
Harrington was a serious thinker who was a man of principle. For instance when he met the Pope he refused to kiss his toe.

Sounds reasonable. It didn't to his holiness. Visitors were expected to kiss the Pope's pinkies as a mark of respect.
Worst career move: Was a bosom buddy of Charles I who loved his company but couldn't stomach his politics.
Best career move: Dedicated a book called *Oceana* to Cromwell in 1656. Oliver, however, turned up his nose and ordered the book to be burnt, until Cromwell's daughter had a word in daddy's ear. In the end Ollie let Harrington publish his book, and even read it himself. He said it gave him a good laugh. *Oceana*'s subject was how to run a Commonwealth.

Odd end: After the Restoration Harrington was jailed and tortured as a supporter of the Commonwealth. Given powerful drugs, he finally went raving bonkers and imagined that he sweated the spirits of flies and bees.

Samuel Cooper

Occupation: Painter.

Dead famous? Are you kidding? He's considered to be one of England's best miniature painters.

Why was he such a shrimp? Not him, the paintings. At the time there was a big fashion in art for mini-portraits, about the size of a large brooch. Perhaps people liked them because you could keep them in your pocket, which was difficult to do with paintings that took up an entire wall.

Best career move: Cooper did a number of miniature portraits including Mrs Cromwell – or Protectoress Joan as her enemies nicknamed her. Cooper's portrait of Oliver shows his warts clearly. Getting his nose on a miniature must have been a real work of art.

Oliver's empire

At home Cromwell's pet poets – Milton and Marvell – were glowing about the Protectorate. Abroad progress was more stormy. Cromwell's dream was to make

England a great seafaring nation again. Let's face it, since the days of the sinking of the Spanish Armada, there hadn't been much to shout about.

Cromwell's foreign policy was called his 'western design'. In a nutshell he wanted to get his greedy hands on the West Indies. Cromwell claimed he would bring godliness to the islands but his real interest was in the rich trade the islands offered.

Only one thing stood in his way – Spain, the old enemy who had the Caribbean trade sewn up. Cromwell's first attempt to attack the Spanish was a shambles. The expedition to the Caribbean island of Hispaniola was led by the naval commander, William Penn. Funnily enough, it was also led by Colonel Robert Venables.

Cromwell should have known having two commanders was a recipe for disaster. When things started to go wrong, they both blamed each other. Here's Venables's miserable tale of woe.

Cromwell was so upset by Venables's miserable failure that he shut himself in his room. He needn't have worried – his navy did capture Jamaica which was a prize worth having. Two years later they defeated the Spanish at the battle of Santa Cruz in the Canary Islands.

England was back in business. It was just like the good old days of the Armada again.

Crowning glory?

Oliver had ended a trade war with the Dutch, made friends with the French, fought the Spanish and gained a foothold in the West Indies. It wasn't bad going for a man who'd hardly set foot outside of East Anglia for his first 40 years.

Yet now, at the ripe old age of 58, he faced the biggest decision of his life. He was living in a palace and being treated like a king by foreign countries. Why not have done with it and call himself a king? A two to one majority in the House of Commons voted in favour of it. What was to stop him?

Cromwell's decision wasn't easy. The crown would strengthen his authority, but was kingship betraying everything he stood for? If we could peek into his diary we'd find he was in two minds – at least.

Oliver's Secret Diary

23rd February 1657

Parliament wants me to become king. What should I do? It'd be nice for Elizabeth to be queen and my children royalty. To say nothing of the £1,300,000 a year that comes with the job. On the other hand what if that upstart Charles II ever wants his crown back? It could be my head on the block – and the chop for my family too.

2nd April

10 p.m. — Told my friends over dinner that I definitely wouldn't become king on any account.

Midnight — Told them I'd be happy to be king.

May 5th

My mind is made up once and for all. It's God's will I become king. I do it not for myself, but for my country. Wonder if I'll look good in purple?

May 6th

Went for a walk in St James's park with my mind made up. By an amazing coincidence bumped into three of my old army pals who just happened to be taking a stroll there too. They told me they'd resign their commands if I accepted the crown. It's clear as day I cannot become king. God forbids it. And I don't much fancy fighting the army either...

King OLIVER the 1st? OLLIE OLLIE REX?

THE RIGHTEOUS ROUNDHEAD

8 MAY 1657

CARRY ON CROWNLESS

Oliver Cromwell has rejected the crown and the chance to enter history as King Oliver I. Cromwell would have been the first ex-army captain ever to sit on the throne. The House of Commons had urged him to take the title of 'King of England, Scotland and Ireland' in a document called 'the Humble Petition and Advice'. But the Protector was too humble to take their advice and said no.

Suspense

For six weeks the country has held its breath waiting to see what the Lord Protector would decide. In the end it was a close run thing. Friends say Cromwell was swayed by his old army chums who hated the idea of having to bow the knee to their former colonel.

The general reaction at home and abroad was amazement. How could anyone in their right mind turn down the crown when it was offered to them on a silver plate? Yet the decision was typical of Cromwell. Typical that he took ages to decide and then did what no one expected. Good or bad, wise or crazy, Cromwell was always his own man.

In any case he only had one more year to live. His life's work was about to come crumbling down on his head. But the head is another story…

OLD OLIVER AND HIS WANDERING HEAD

On 25 May 1657 Oliver arrived by boat at Westminster. In Westminster Hall a purple robe was placed round his shoulders and he was given the sword of state and a heavy gold sceptre. The trumpets sounded and the people cheered. Had Oliver decided to be crowned king after all?

MAYBE I COULD JUST TRY IT?

No, it was only the ceremony to install him as Lord Protector for a second time.

By now a big question-mark hung over Cromwell. Since the Civil War the country had effectively been ruled by one powerful man. What would happen when great Cromwell turned up his toes? The question was an urgent one. Take a look at doddery Ollie at age 58 and you'll see why.

Oliver was not the man he used to be. All those long campaigns and battlescars had taken their toll. His signature on letters (Oliver Protector) had once looked like this:

Now it looked more like this:

According to one visitor Oliver's coat was 'not worth three shillings a yard' which suggests he'd reverted to his old habit of dressing like a country cousin. More worrying were the signs that his health was breaking down. There were even rumours among the royalists that the Protector was as mad as a March hare.

Some say he is ... like one distracted, and in these fits he will run about the house and into the garden.

These rumours were probably more hopeful than accurate. Yet there's no doubt that Oliver's body was showing signs of old age, even if his mind was sharp. More and more he spent time with his doctors discussing pills and potions.

If we could read his doctor's case book we'd discover the long list of his problems.

Dr McGinlay's Casebook

Patient: O. Cromwell - Lord Protector
11 December 1655
Patient complains of 'agonies' from the stone in his bladder. Have written to an excellent fellow in Paris who claims to work miracles with this kind of thing. Sadly the great doctor won't cross the Channel for less than a thousand francs paid in advance. My Lord Protector roared like a bear when I told him. I took this to mean 'No'.

10 January 1656

Patient complains of gout, a boil on the chest and Bladder Stone. (Truly he is a walking medical textbook!)

Advised my Lord Cromwell to ride around the park in his coach to see if the bumping motion will disturb the stone. Otherwise we could always try cutting it out. This might work, though I have lost one or two under the knife.

WARTS AND ALL ~ DEADLY DOCTORS

There was no National Health Service in Cromwell's day. Treatment was a hit and miss affair. Usually it was more miss than hit. (Some experts today reckon that Oliver actually suffered from a form of malaria.) If you were rich and important like Oliver, then you'd have your own doctor (not always a good thing). If you were poor you were lucky to get any treatment at all. Any poor soul who got the plague could stay in a wooden cabin called a 'pest house'. They paid two pence a day for the privilege of dying in a shed, well away from anyone else. In any case, if you got the plague you weren't expected to live long.

When you finally dropped dead, old women called 'searchers' came to search your body and report the cause of death to the parish clerk. Here's a list of reported deaths from 1650. As you'll see the 'searchers' had pretty vague ideas about fatal illnesses.

11-18th January 1650 - Deaths reported in London.	
PLAGUE 0	KILLED 28 (one by a piece of falling timber in Timber Street and 27 by the blast of Gunpowder)
ABORTIVE (Died at birth) 15	
COUGH 2	SCURVY 1
DROWNED AT ST JAMES DUKE PLACE 1	SMALLPOX 11
	TEETH 15
GRIEF 1	WIND 2
PALSY 1	VOMITING 1

If dying of bad teeth or an attack of wind sounds daft, some of the cures that seventeenth century doctors prescribed were even crazier. Burns and bruises, for instance, were supposed to be helped by a soothing dressing of horse dung, and the recipes for keeping away the dreaded plague were even more revolting:

Take the brains of a young man who has died a violent death. Mix with the nerves, the arteries and pith of the backbone. Leave to ferment for 6 months. Take a drop a day to keep the plague away.

Pass the veg

Many illnesses were probably caused by people failing to eat a healthy diet. Poor children often suffered from rickets (where their limbs grew crooked) because of a lack of calcium.

Puritans like Oliver's wife, Elizabeth, believed in a simple diet because 'the Kingdom of God is not meat and drink but righteousness and peace'. However don't imagine that Mrs Cromwell's idea of a simple diet was a healthy salad ... she liked to give her hubbie:

MARROW PUDDING, FOLLOWED BY HOG'S LIVER AND SAUSAGES FOR DINNER.

No wonder Oliver was no stick insect!

Meat was the main dish of the age and dishes included beef, venison (deer), mutton, chicken or brawn. Vegetables rarely appeared on the plate as people believed they gave you wind. Fruit, however, was readily available and two new fruits – bananas and pineapples – were first introduced to Britain during the Commonwealth. However, nobody was rash enough to try eating a weird-looking fruit like a banana raw. As for pineapples, most people thought they looked decidedly dangerous and treated them as ornaments!

Son of Ollie

Despite his wife's home cooking, Oliver continued to go downhill in old age. As his health got worse, the question of who would replace him became more and more urgent. Normally dying kings simply passed on the crown to their oldest son (or daughter if they didn't have sons). But Oliver wasn't a king, so the question of his successor was an open one. Parliament had agreed that Oliver could name his own choice, but there lay the problem. Oliver, remember, could be a great ditherer when it came to big decisions.

There were two main rivals for the job.

Richard Cromwell
CLAIM: OLDEST SON.
WEAK POINTS: A TOTAL LOSER.

Henry Cromwell
CLAIM: STRONG CHARACTER LIKE HIS DAD AND EXPERIENCE OF RULING IN IRELAND.
WEAK POINTS: YOUNGER SON, SECOND IN PECKING ORDER.

Henry was by far the better man for the job of Protector. Not only was he tougher than his elder brother, but also he'd shown in Ireland that he could handle a difficult job.

Richard by comparison was a hopeless softie. His hobbies were hawking, horse-racing, hunting and running up bills. Poor Dick had the nature of 'a country peasant' and none of his father's greatness. His only talent was having unfortunate accidents. When the staircase collapsed at the London Banqueting House, who was standing on it? When a coach got dragged along by its runaway horses, who got injured? Asking Dick to rule the country was just asking for trouble.

So who should it be – dead-loss Dick or hunky Henry? There was obviously no contest. But Oliver chose Richard, who promptly lived up to his accident-prone reputation by losing the Commonwealth. No wonder they called him Tumbledown Dick.

Dead famous

The end was near for Oliver and the signs didn't look good. In the summer of 1658 a whale was sighted in the River Thames near Greenwich. After a horrid groan it ran ashore and died. Londoners were amazed at the sight of the 60 foot giant and must have wondered if that other giant at Whitehall was next to die.

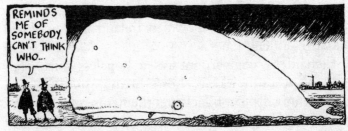

In September 1658 a great storm swept across England as the Protector lay ill. Huge oak trees were uprooted, roofs were torn off houses, ships sank at sea. Church towers came crashing down and the wind came howling over the Thames. Everyone saw it as an omen of great disasters to come and from Cromwell's point of view they weren't far wrong. Great Ironsides was dying.

On Thursday, 2 September, the Council of State gathered at Oliver's bedside. He still hadn't got round to naming his successor and time was running out. Oliver was far gone. Twice they had to put the name of Richard to him before he nodded his answer. Oliver lasted through the night, often talking to himself and God. When he was offered a drink he replied:

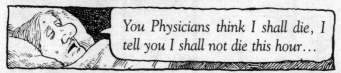

It is not my design to drink or to sleep, but it is my design is to make what haste I can to be gone.

History books sometimes record these as Oliver's last words. In fact they weren't. Later that morning Oliver turned to his doctors and said:

You Physicians think I shall die, I tell you I shall not die this hour...

Even in death Old Noll had to be right – he lasted some hours longer and died in the afternoon when he was good and ready. Oddly, the date he died – 3 September – was the same date as his famous victory over Charles II at

Worcester. Later royalist pamphlets suggested he'd made a pact with the Devil to win at Worcester which was redeemed seven years later at his death. He was 59 years old and had ruled England as Protector for five years. Curiously, what killed this giant of man was the same as what killed Goliath – one little stone. In Cromwell's case the stone was in his bladder. As a famous French philosopher, Blaise Pascal, remarked years later:

Because of this small piece of gravel, he is dead, his family is cast down, all is peaceful and the king is restored.

But that's leaping ahead a bit. First Oliver had to be buried.

THE RIGHTEOUS ROUNDHEAD

23 NOVEMBER 1658

OLIVER GOES OUT IN STYLE

He may have scorned a crown but Oliver Cromwell was buried like a king today. People crowded the streets and hung from windows and rooftops to see the procession go past. Some had come from as far away as Cornwall to see the great man laid to rest. 'People were up in wonderment and admiration,' said an eyewitness. 'They were gazing and hurrying as if some marvellous and great thing had happened to them.'

Dead expensive

One wonders what plain Old Noll would have made of his own funeral. The man who once dismissed Parliament in his old grey stockings was spared no expense. The procession was so long it took seven hours to travel the one mile to Westminster Abbey. Reports put Cromwell's funeral bill between £30,000 and £60,000 which makes King James I's funeral look dirt cheap!

Six plumed horses covered in black velvet pulled Oliver's hearse. On the hearse lay a splendid effigy of Cromwell carved out of wood. The wax face had coloured glass eyes which could actually open and close. Onlookers also spotted that Oliver's effigy wore a richly jewelled crown. For once Cromwell was in no position to argue!

Cromwell was never a simple man. Even in his death people couldn't agree about him. Some thought that his funeral was the least he deserved, others claimed it was a shocking waste of money. Predictably, Puritans looked down their noses at all the pomp and ceremony. Some even threw mud at Cromwell's coat of arms over the gate of Somerset House. Royalists, meanwhile, were delighted.

The joyfullest funeral I ever saw, for there were none that cried but dogs.

Hero or villain?

Cromwell was someone who divided opinion all his life. No one can deny that he was a great man. How many country farmers have risen to be the ruler of three countries? But the question remains: was Oliver a hero or a villain? Rude Roundheads and dashing Cavaliers held their own opinions.

HE WAS A HERO **AND** HE WAS HUMBLE!

HE HAD A GREAT HEART!

HE LED A REVOLUTION!

HE REFUSED THE CROWN!

A TWO-FACED TYRANT WHO DRESSED LIKE A PIG-FARMER!

GREAT NOSE MORE LIKE!

HE BEHEADED THE KING!

HIS HEAD WAS TOO BIG FOR IT!

How can you sum up a man like Oliver Cromwell? He could be cruel to his enemies and kind to his friends. He was a solemn Puritan and a daft practical joker. One royalist writer, the Earl of Clarendon, called him: 'A brave, bad man'. Maybe that's as good a summary of Cromwell as any. Whether he was bad or good depended on whose side you were on. But even if you hated him you had to admire him.

After Oliver

Oliver was dead but his story isn't quite over yet. What became of the Commonwealth that he'd worked so hard to create? Remember he left his eldest son, Richard, in charge of the country. And remember what Richard was like.

Richard started off by going to Westminster in his newly built coach and calling a Parliament. So far so good. He didn't even trip over his coat-tails when he stood up to make his big speech. He simply asked everyone to make this 'a happy Parliament', but this Parliament turned out to be as friendly as a seventeenth century football match.

Within eight months the whole Commonwealth had collapsed about poor Dick's ears. Unlike his dad he never had the support of the army and soon fled abroad to France. It all happened very quickly. Without Oliver there was no one to hold the country on course. All Charles II had to do was sit tight and wait to be invited back by Parliament. That was exactly what happened.

The rowdy Restoration

Charles landed at Dover on 29 May 1660. There was wild rejoicing all over the country. Here's how royalist John Evelyn described the scene:

> *This day came in His Majestie Charles the Second to London ... with a Triumph of above 2000 horse and foot (infantry), brandishing their swords and shouting with unexpressible joy: The ways strewed with flowers, the bells ringing, the streets hung with Tapestry, fountains running with wine ... the windows and balconies all set with Ladies, Trumpets, Music and people flocking the streets... I stood in the Strand and beheld it and blessed God.*

Oliver must have been turning in his grave. It looked as if the revolution had turned out to be little more than a hiccup in history. Chopping off Charles I's head had never been popular and the Commonwealth had never won the hearts of the people. With the Merry Monarch, Charles II, on the throne, people could once again take a stroll on Sundays, go to the theatre and tuck into their Christmas dinner. That was reason enough to give three cheers for the king.

In the end none of the questions that had started the Civil War had actually been settled. Charles II claimed to rule by divine right, just like his daffy old dad. The relationship between king and parliament was still a muddle and the Anglican church had made a comeback. So what had been the point of it all?

On the face of it Oliver's revolution looked like a rotten flop. But it hadn't all been for nothing. Parliament had shown it wasn't going to be treated like the king's pet poodle. For the first time in history it had shown its teeth. After the Civil War no king could imagine they were free to rule any way they pleased. Oliver Cromwell had shown that kings were there to serve their subjects – and if they didn't they'd get a sharp reminder.

Rest in pieces

As for Old Coppernose himself he wasn't allowed to rest quietly. Generally Charles II was prepared to forgive and forget but not in the case of those who signed his dad's death warrant. The top name on the list was Oliver Cromwell's. Already Oliver was starting to become a legend. Some said his body had been thrown in the Thames. Other stories said it lay in the coffin of Charles I at Windsor, or even that it had been 'carried away in the tempest the night before'.

This was all codswallop of course. Cromwell's body in fact lay in a tomb in Westminster Abbey – but not for long. Royalists weren't going to be cheated of their revenge on Cromwell – even if he was dead as a dodo. They decided Old Noll should be dug up to take his punishment.

On the night of 29 January 1661 – eight months after the Restoration – royalist soldiers rudely dragged Oliver's body from its resting place. It spent the night on the bar of the Red Lion Inn in Holborn (and wasn't even offered a drink).

Fittingly, the next day was the twelfth anniversary of Charles I getting the chop. Oliver's body was dragged on a sledge to Tyburn while the ugly crowd pelted it with stones. There it hung on the gallows from nine in the morning until six at night. (It was joined by the bodies of Ireton, Cromwell's son-in-law, and Judge Bradshaw, who tried Charles I.) If that wasn't gruesome enough, Cromwell's corpse was then beheaded. Unfortunately the London hangman at the time, Edward Dun, wasn't so handy with an axe. It took seven or eight blows to finish the job.

I THINK HE'S QUITE DEFINITELY DEAD NOW!

Cromwell's body was flung into a pit at Tyburn. If you go to Marble Arch in London you can stand at the exact spot where the gallows were. Spectators took away several of Cromwell's body bits as souvenirs – fingers, toes and one of Oliver's ears went missing. As for his head, it was held up for the crowd to see. But no one knew that it had just begun one of the strangest journeys in history.

The last Roundhead

1661 Six days after getting the chop Oliver's head is displayed on a 25-foot spike on top of Westminster Hall. The noggins of Ireton and Bradshaw keep it company.

WELL, ISN'T THIS FUN?

It stays there for 24 years until…

1685 During a violent storm the spike breaks and Oliver's head gets blown down. It nearly hits a sentry, sheltering from the storm. When he gets over the shock, he takes the head home and stuffs it up his chimney. Meanwhile half of London is looking for the man who's nabbed Oliver's noddle.

1702 On his deathbed the soldier leaves his wife an unexpected gift.

UM… THANKS DEAR, IT'S JUST WHAT I ALWAYS WANTED…

1710 The head is flogged off by the soldier's family. It next turns up in a collection of curiosities. Du Puy's show includes waxworks, musical instruments, weird footwear and the embalmed head of Oliver Cromwell.

1773 The head is sold to the Russell family, who just happen to be descendants of Cromwell. It falls into the hands of Samuel Russell, a failed comic actor and successful drunk. Skint Samuel tries to sell his ancestor's head to Sidney Sussex College, Cambridge (where Cromwell was once a student). When the offer is turned down Russell shows off the head on a local market stall.

1787 Cromwell's sliced loaf is 'picked up as bargain for £118' by James Cox, a jeweller and showman.

1799 Cox sells it at a tidy profit for £230 to the three Hughes brothers. They advertise their treasure in the *Morning Chronicle* newspaper: '*The Real Embalmed Head of the Powerful and Renowned Usurper, Oliver Cromwell is now exhibited at 5 Mead Court, Bond St. (where the rattlesnake was shown last year). Tickets half a crown.*'

1813 Does the head carry a curse? The Hughes brothers all come to sticky ends. One is mugged by a highwayman, the second drowns, the third falls off his horse and dies. Just a coincidence?

1814 The much-travelled bonce is bought by the Hughes' family doctor – Josiah Wilkinson. The dotty doc keeps it in a red silk-lined box to show his patients.

1911 The head goes on display at the Royal Archaeological Institute in London. Two other heads claiming to be Cromwell's appear in the same collection. The rivals are unmasked as rotten fakes.

1932 Experts at London University examine Old Noll's noddle to see if it's genuine. It has brown leathery skin, traces of red hair and has been embalmed, chopped off and rammed on a spike about 300 years ago. One ear is missing and the nose is squashed, where it fell off the block.

1960 The head stays in the Wilkinson family until the owner offers it to Oliver's old college again. This time it's accepted. In order to avoid being pestered by horrible head-hunters the college authorities decide to hide the mouldy relic. Putting it in a biscuit tin, they bury it somewhere in the grounds of Sidney Sussex College. Where exactly? Ahh, that's a secret!

Experts are still arguing today whether the mysterious buried head is the actual nut of Oliver Cromwell. Even in modern times people continue to come up with rival claims. In 1979 a Lincolnshire man unearthed a skull which he swore was the legendary Roundhead's head. The owner was told it was far too small to be the head of Cromwell. He protested: